My COMPUTeachER

The Computer Book for Everyone

Paul Rallion, MAE, NBCT

My COMPUTeachER
The Computer Book for Everyone

This book is available at:
www.paulrallion.com

ISBN: 978-1-105-56029-3 (sc)
ISBN: 978-1-329-23983-8 (ebk)

Printed in the United States of America
Rev. date: 06/17/2016

Dedications

To All My Students: Past, Present, and Future

I dedicate this book to all my students: past, present, and future. Their presence and participation in my classroom has made my teaching worthwhile. With this book I'd like to reach students that I won't have the fortune to meet.

—Paul

Contents

Introduction

Throughout the years, many people have asked me questions regarding computer applications. As a computer instructor, I decided that publishing some of them (not necessarily in question format) might have a high interest value. This book is a comprehensive collection of all the handouts I have developed through my last 20 years in the classroom.

The handouts in this book represent the bulk of my classes. Following each handout, there is a suggested class project or exercise, a homework assignment, and a sample quiz. The answers to some of the questions are found directly on the handouts, while others require deductive reasoning. I have added a few questions that ask for an opinion, and of course, those answers would be neither right nor wrong.

The goal of this book is to provide you with valuable information you can use right away. As you read these handouts, consider this:

• **If you're a teacher:** How do you use technology in the classroom? You can use many of the programs explored in these handouts to enrich your curriculum. If you would like some of this material to become part of your teaching repertoire, feel free to modify class projects or homework and quiz questions.

• **If you're a parent:** You can use these handouts to explore and enjoy your computer more. Perhaps there is a program you would like to know more about. I hope these handouts will be beneficial to you.

• **If you're a student:** Most of what I teach in my computer class is in these handouts. They contain important concepts and tips that you can use throughout your journey as a student and beyond.

• **If you're a professional in another field:** The productivity software covered here is used in most fields of work. There is other software that is recreational in nature. In either case, computer programs can be enjoyed more when understood more deeply.

Disclaimer

Due to the nature of the Internet and computer development, some commands, shortcuts, or Web addresses contained in this book, may have changed since publication and may no longer be valid. The information in this book is for educational purposes only. Nothing herein should be interpreted as personalized advice. None of the information in this book is guaranteed to be correct, and anything written here should be considered subject to independent verification. The author does not take any responsibility for any opinions or ideas expressed in this book. The author does not assume any liability as a result of the use of the information presented herein. Under no circumstances will the author be responsible for incidental or consequential damages or direct or indirect damages that result from your use of the information in this book.

HANDOUT # 01
Computer Basics
WWW.PAULRALLION.COM

Objective: You will learn what a computer is, a short history, and the types of computers.

What is a Computer?

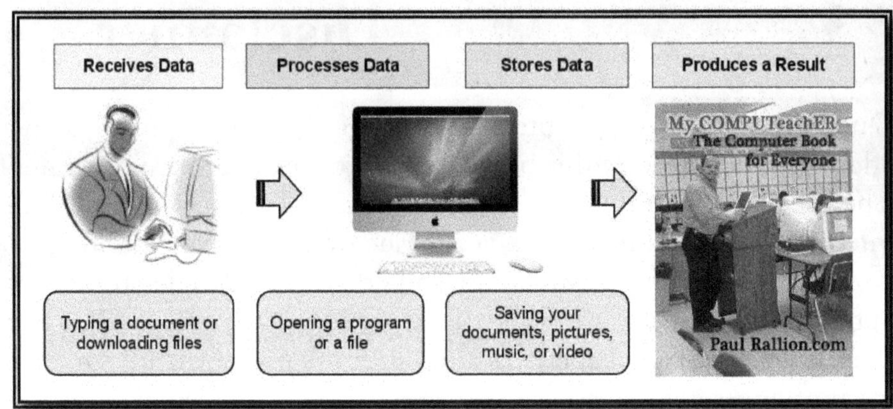

➢ A computer is an electronic device to which you enter or input data, it processes data, it stores data, and it gives you the desired result or output.

History of the Computer:

➢ The computer era began with Charles Babbage in the 1860's. He invented a mechanical calculator. The ENIAC (Electronic Numerical Integrator and Computer) was part of the first generation of computers powered by vacuum tubes in the 1940's. They were temperature-sensitive, expensive, and difficult to repair. These inventions have allowed us to enjoy computers today: the transistor (1947), integrated circuits (1960's), and microprocessors (1970's). The first personal computers became available as follows: The Altair (1974), Apple II (1977), IBM (1981), Macintosh (1984), IBM with Windows (1985). (Winters, Moore, Cambridge Educational 2008).

Computer Applications: ➢ Computers are used in a great number of ways: to type letters, to make tables, charts, to draw, to communicate, etc. Can you name a few more?

Types of Computers

➢ There are different types of computers:

The **microcomputer**, also called personal computer or PC (insert at left), is used at home or at the office. The desktop PC is becoming less popular (refer to the next section), but also less expensive as manufacturing technology becomes more efficient.

The **notebook computer**, also called laptop (insert at right), has similar capabilities to the PC. It is smaller, portable and wireless. It has become more popular than the desktop PC. The **netbook computer** is a new, smaller version of the notebook computer.

The **mainframe computer,** also called server, is larger and more powerful than a microcomputer. Mainframe computers are used for centralized storage and management of large amounts of data (insert at left). Large organizations such as banks, hospitals, universities, etc., use computer servers to store and manage their customers' data. You can withdraw money from your bank account at one bank location, and all other bank branches will have that information updated instantly.

Class Project # 01
Computer Basics
WWW.PAULRALLION.COM

➢ Read the handout and draw examples of how the computer performs the functions described. Do a research on the history of computers. Look up the acronym: ENIAC. What kind of storage devices have been available?

Homework # 01
Computer Basics
WWW.PAULRALLION.COM

1.- What are four things all computers do?
2.- Describe the types of computers
3.- Make a list of 10 uses of a computer (NOT from the handout)

Sample Quiz # 01
Computer Basics
WWW.PAULRALLION.COM

1.- Give an example of a computer producing a result.
2.- Give an example of a computer input device.
3.- Computers used for centralized storage, processing, and management of large amounts of data:
4.- What is one way we use computers today (NOT from the handout)?

HANDOUT # 02
Keyboarding
WWW.PAULRALLION.COM

Objective: You will learn keyboarding, the correct way to type.

QWERTY Keyboard Layout

➢ Our current keyboard layout was designed about 150 years ago to prevent keys from jamming in a typewriter (picture at right). This layout is here to stay, so it makes sense to memorize the key locations.

➢ Keyboarding is the ability to enter text by using the correct fingers without looking at the keys –one of the most useful computer skills! Place you fingers over the home row keys:

a, s, d, f, (left hand), ---- j, k, l, ; (right hand).

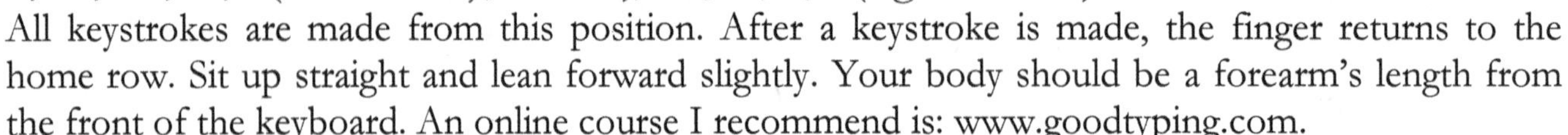
All keystrokes are made from this position. After a keystroke is made, the finger returns to the home row. Sit up straight and lean forward slightly. Your body should be a forearm's length from the front of the keyboard. An online course I recommend is: www.goodtyping.com.

International Keyboard Set Up (to type accents and ñ's):

➢ <u>For Windows:</u> Control Panel ⇨ Clock, Language, Region ⇨ Regional & Language Options ⇨ Change Keyboards or other input methods ⇨ Change Keyboards ⇨ General tab: Select English (United States) - United States - International. Click Ok.

To type an accent: type the ' key and then the letter. To type the ñ, type the ~ key and then the n.

➢ <u>For Mac:</u> Press and hold the Option key + the letter e key, then type the letter you wish accented. For ñ, press and hold the Option key + the letter n key, then type the letter n again.

Avoiding Physical Injury:

➢ To reduce the effect of Carpal Tunnel Syndrome, learn to use the mouse with BOTH hands, and alternate between them every few months. It may seem hard at first, but it's worth trying.

➢ To avoid eye fatigue, take visual breaks. Look at and focus for a few seconds on a distant object (as far as you can) and then turn to look at something close for a few seconds. Repeat.

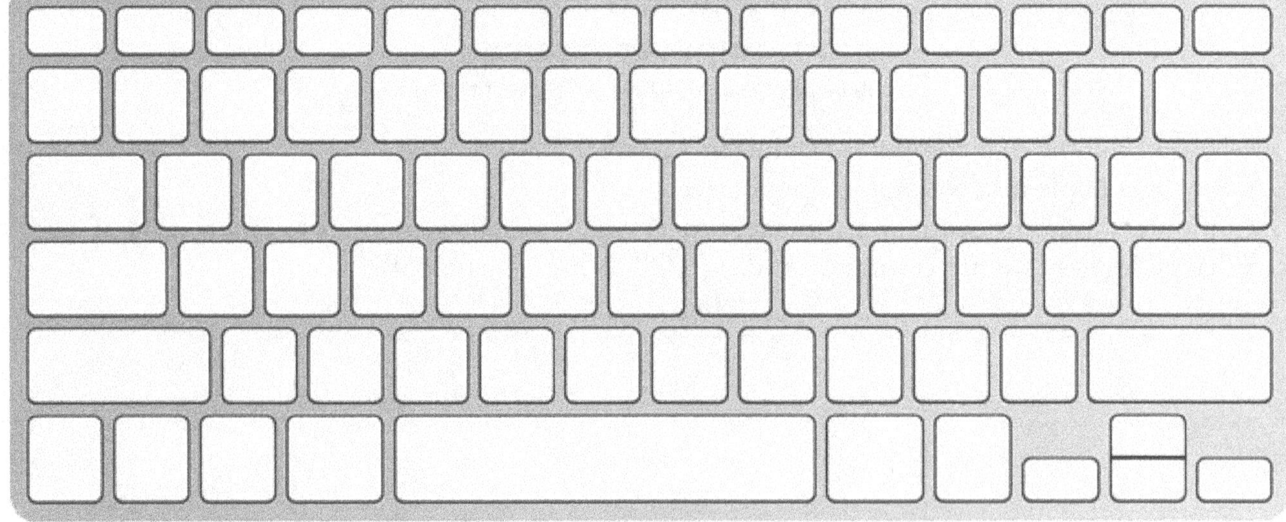

Class Project # 02
Keyboarding
WWW.PAULRALLION.COM

➢ Find a free typing tutorial online and practice your typing skills. The one I receommend is www.goodtyping.com. Remember, DO NOT look at the keyboard!

Homework # 02
Keyboarding
WWW.PAULRALLION.COM

1.- Which keys are the "home row"?
2.- Why is it called the "home row"?
3.- Describe the correct Keyboarding Posture.
4.- What are some things you can do to lessen physical injury?

Sample Quiz # 02
Keyboarding
WWW.PAULRALLION.COM

1.- Which keys are the "home row"?
2.- The ability to type using the correct fingers without looking at the keys is called:
3.- Touch typing is also called:
4.- The correct typing position refers to your:

Handout # 03
Computer Drawing
WWW.PAULRALLION.COM

Objective: You will learn how to use a Drawing® program.

Computer Drawing®:

➢ Drawing® is a program used to create simple shapes such as rectangles, circles, lines, and polygons (see insert at right). You can combine these shapes to create designs –such as a map or a quick sketch. A drawing is made of "objects" – separate elements such as rectangles, lines, and text, as well as paint and spreadsheet frames. An object has eight handles (eight dots around it) when you select it (click on it). These handles are used to resize the object. To move the object around, click and hold your mouse anywhere inside the object. You can make copies of your object by going to: *Edit,* and selecting *Copy*. Then go to *Edit*, and select *Paste.*

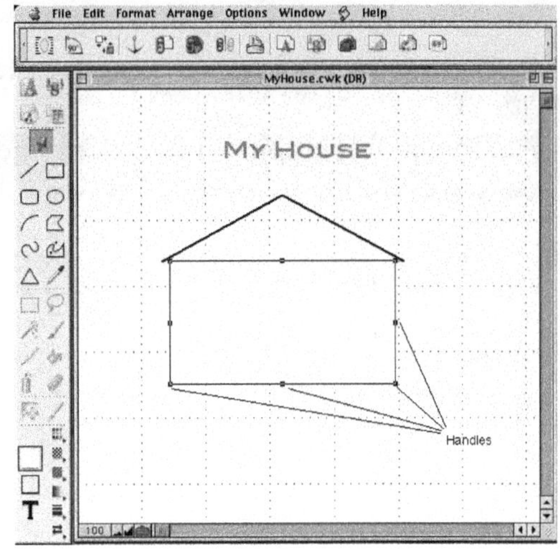

Using the Tool Panel (below):

➢ The tool panel contains icons that represent the tools used to work in Drawing®. You use these tools to create, select, move, resize, and reshape objects. For a description of each tool just place your mouse over any icon.

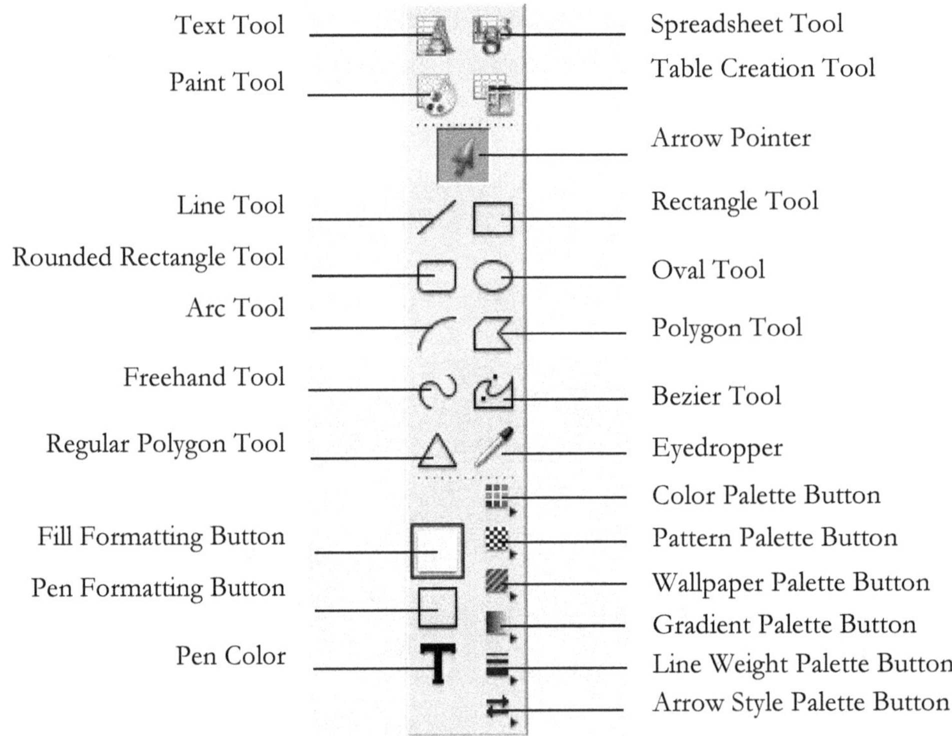

Class Project # 03
Computer Drawing
WWW.PAULRALLION.COM

- Draw a sketch of your neighborhood. Label street names and main buildings.

Homework # 03
Computer Drawing
WWW.PAULRALLION.COM

1.- What can you create with a Drawing program?
2.- What is a drawing made of?
3.- How do you make a copy of an object?
4.- How do you get a description of a tool?

Sample Quiz # 03
Computer Drawing
WWW.PAULRALLION.COM

1.- A drawing is made of:_________ (simple shapes like rectangles, circles, etc.)
2.- What do you call the dots around the simple shapes:
3.- How many dots are there in a rectangle or square in Drawing?
4.- How do you make your work area wider?

Handout # 04

Parts of the Computer

WWW.PAULRALLION.COM

Objective: You will learn the parts of a personal computer, or a PC. You will learn what software is, and what hardware is.

What is Software?

➢ Software is a set of instructions (programs) and data that a computer uses to do its job. For example: Microsoft Word, Microsoft Excel, Microsoft PowerPoint, Painting, Drawing, Electronic Mail (e-mail), Google Docs, etc.

What is Hardware?

➢ Hardware is the materials and physical components the computer is made of: The monitor (screen), keyboard, mouse, CPU (Central Processing Unit), USB flashdrives, etc.

What is the Operating System?

➢ The Operating System is a type of software that allows the computer hardware and other computer software "talk to each other," to be able to function. Examples of Operating Systems are: Mac OS X®, or Windows® 10, Linux.

The Parts of a Computer

➢ The Computer consists of several parts:
CPU: Central Processing Unit. The CPU contains some or all of the following:

- HD: Hard Drive, - CDW-ROM: Compact Disk Writable – Read Only Memory,
- DVD: Digital Video Disk, - USB (Universal Serial Bus) connections, video outputs.

Keyboard, Mouse, Monitor, Digital Camera, Printer, Scanner.

Input or Output?

➢ If you use a device to send information to the CPU, it is called an input. For example: when you press a key on the keyboard, information is flowing into the CPU, so the keyboard would be an input device. Label the following pictures, including whether they're input or output:

CLASS PROJECT # 04
Parts of the Computer
WWW.PAULRALLION.COM

- Redraw the parts of the computer in Drawing and label each part.

HOMEWORK # 04
Parts of the Computer
WWW.PAULRALLION.COM

1.- What is Software?
2.- What is Hardware?
3.- What is an Operating System?
4.- Label the The Parts of a Computer (include Inputs and Outputs)

SAMPLE QUIZ # 04
Parts of the Computer
WWW.PAULRALLION.COM

1.- A set of instructions that tells the computer what to do is called:
2.- The materials and physical components of the computer are called:
3.- The keyboard and mouse, are they Input or Output?
4.- The printer, is it Input or Output?

HANDOUT # 05
Computer Painting
WWW.PAULRALLION.COM

Objective: You will learn how to use a Painting® program.

➤ Painting® is a program used to create simple shapes such as rectangles, circles, lines, and polygons (see picture). You can also create airbrush or brushstroke effects, tint colors, or create "hand-painted" artwork. A popular use of this program is to work with scanned pictures, i.e.: you can add or delete stuff from pictures, decorate them, etc.

Using the Tool Panel (below):

➤ The tool panel contains icons that represent the tools used to work in Painting®. You use these tools to paint images, draw objects, and change the appearance of objects. Below is the tool panel with the name of each icon. For a description of each tool, go to: *Help*, select: *Show Balloons*, and place your mouse over any icon.

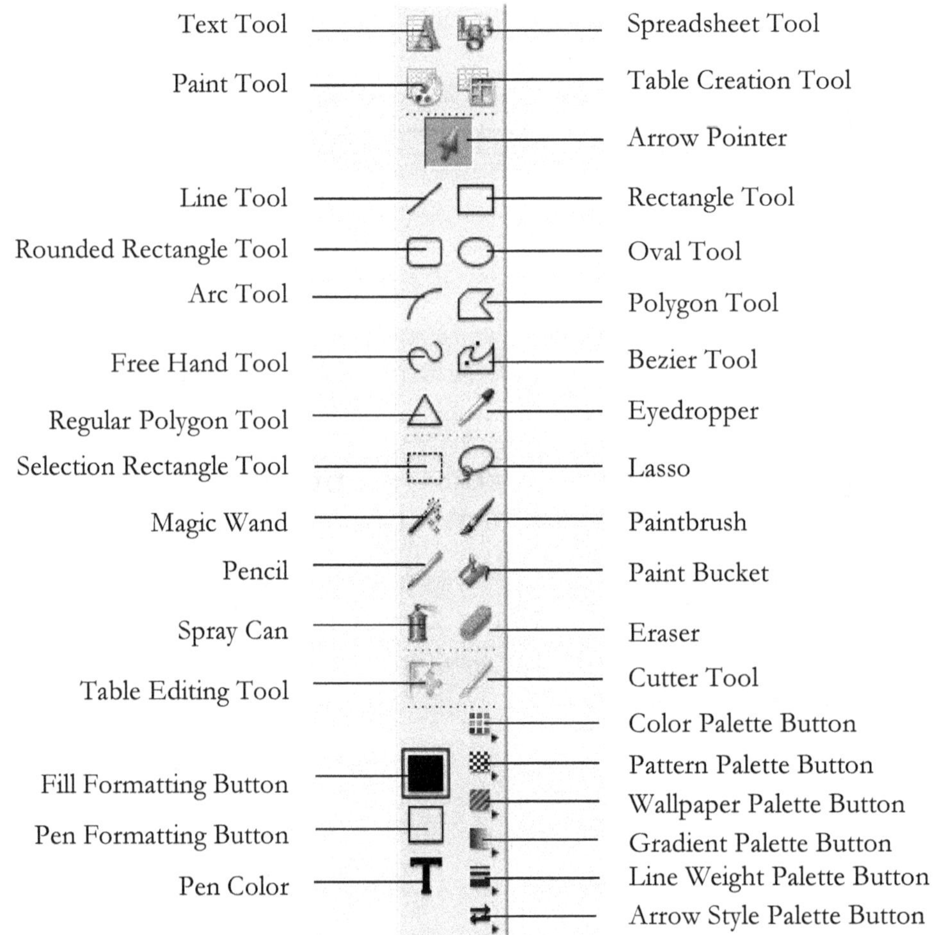

Class Project # 05
Computer Painting
WWW.PAULRALLION.COM

➢ Find a picture of a landmark, from anywhere in the world, and reproduce from scratch, with your Painting program. Use as many as the tools as possible to make it as close to the original as possible.

Homework # 05
Computer Painting
WWW.PAULRALLION.COM

1.- What can you do with a Painting program?
2.- Which tools are now available that were not available in Drawing?
3.- Why do you think a popular use of Painting is to work with scanned pictures?

Sample Quiz # 05
Computer Painting
WWW.PAULRALLION.COM

1.- Name a popular use of this computer program:
2.- What do you place over a tool on the toolbar to get its description?
3.- With this program you can: paint images, draw objects, and:
4.- How do you make your work area wider?

Handout # 06
Computer Desktop
WWW.PAULRALLION.COM

Objective: You will learn to describe the computer desktop, and explain the difference between the Microsoft Windows desktop and the Apple Mac desktop.

What is the Desktop?
➢ The desktop is the first screen you see when the operating system (Windows or Mac OS - Operating System) is up and fully running. It is called desktop because the icons symbolize real objects on a real desktop. Icons are shortcuts to programs or files, or other functions.

What is GUI?
➢ GUI stands for Graphical User Interface. It makes a computer easier to use by freeing you from memorizing complicated text commands. Instead, you point and click with your mouse, or some other input device, to activate programs and commands.

Microsoft Windows Desktop
➢ The Windows® Desktop has the icons on the left by default, but you can move them around. The taskbar is at the bottom by default, but you can place it on any side. The taskbar shows you which programs or files are open. To go from one program or file to another, click its button on the taskbar. You can also do this: Hold "Alt," and press "Tab." The taskbar has more icons which are shortcuts to other functions or programs. Some applications, such as Virus protection programs are shown next to the clock.

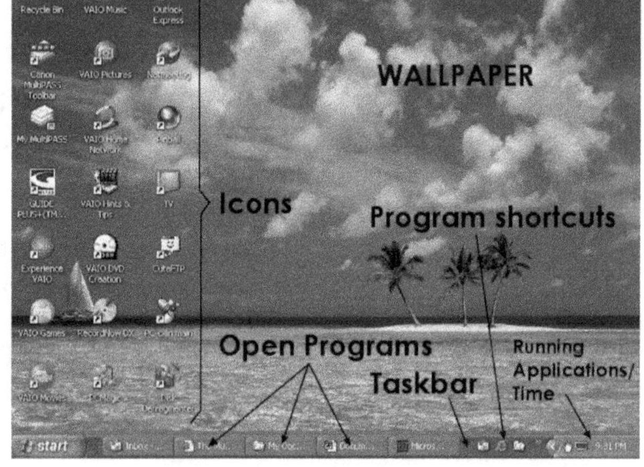

Apple Mac Desktop
➢ The Macintosh OSX® ("O-S-10") Desktop has the icons on the right by default, but you can also move them around. The menu bar is fixed at the top. The "Dock" contains icons to open programs, documents, folders, and minimized windows. You can also see which programs or files are open. To go from one program to another hold "Apple Command," and press "Tab." The open programs have a small arrow under its icon. You can customize the size of the dock, as well as its position on the desktop.

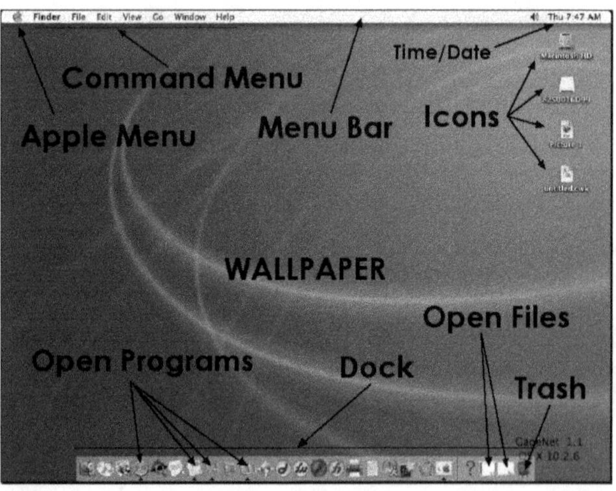

Tip: Place only a few icons on your desktop. An excessive number of icons on your desktop not only may slow down your computer but it may also make the desktop look messy.

CLASS PROJECT # 06

Computer Desktop

WWW.PAULRALLION.COM

➢ Redraw both desktops and label its parts. Discuss the difference between the two desktops: Mac and Windows.

HOMEWORK # 06

Computer Desktop

WWW.PAULRALLION.COM

1.- Why does GUI make a computer easier to use?
2.- Why is it called the "Desktop"?
3.- Make a table of differences between the Mac and the Windows desktop.
4.- Which desktop do you prefer, Windows or Mac? Why?

SAMPLE QUIZ # 06

Computer Desktop

WWW.PAULRALLION.COM

1.- Shortcuts to programs or files are called:
2.- In Windows, where can you see which programs are open?
3.- In Macintosh, where can you see which programs are open?
4.- In Macintosh, what do open programs have under its icon?

Handout # 07
Scanning Pictures
WWW.PAULRALLION.COM

Objective: You will learn how to scan pictures so you can modify them or use them in your work, i.e.: a report, a web page, etc.

What is a scanner?

➢ A scanner is an input device that "takes a <u>digital</u> picture of a document or a photograph," either in black-and-white or color.

Steps to scan!

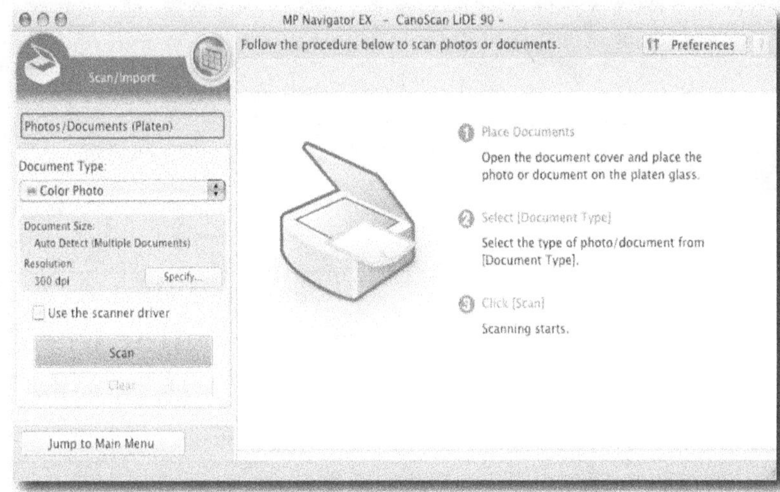

➢ Connect your scanner to your computer (wired or wireless), and follow these steps to scan:

1) Place your picture face down on the scanner's glass.
2) Open the scanner's software and insert a USB flashdrive
3) Click **Scan** – click Exit
4) Click **Save** – type a name for your picture
5) Click **Browse** – click MrRallion – click **Open**
6) Click **Save** – click **Close** – click **Clear – Ok**
7) Eject USB drive – take to your computer
8) Plug in USB drive on your computer
9) Click icon & drag your scanned picture to Pictures folder.

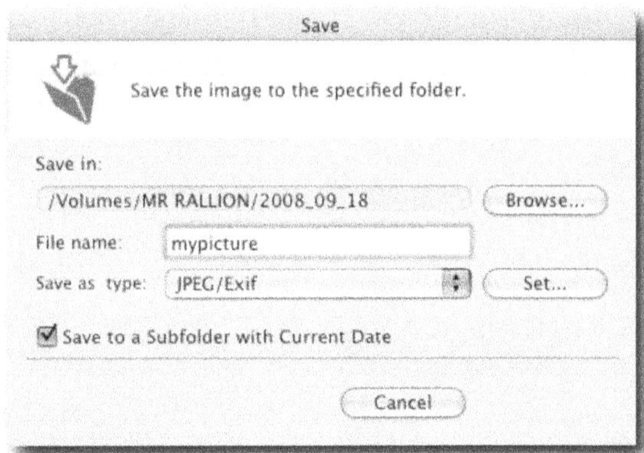

Your file is saved by default with a .jpg extension. JPG stands for Joint Photographer's Group, and is the preferred format for pictures.

Picture File Settings:

➢ You should set your settings to "Color Photo," 300 dpi (dots per inch) resolution. If you want to re-print the picture you want a Higher Resolution. If you want to email the picture file to someone, you want to select a Lower Resolution.

Now what?

➢ You can now make changes to your picture with Painting, you can add it to text in word processing, or in a web page design program, or just print it out.

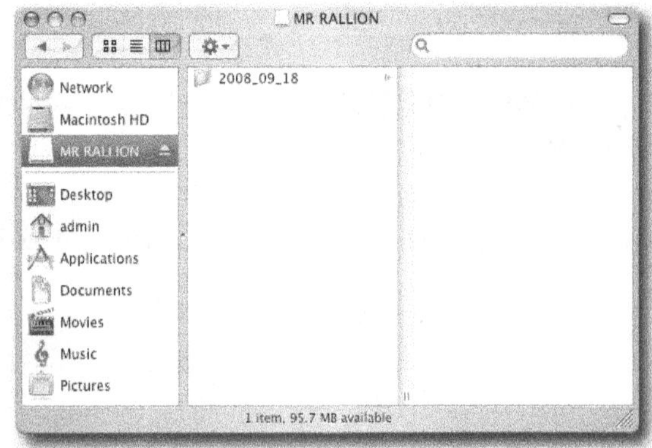

Class Project # 07
Scanning Pictures
WWW.PAULRALLION.COM

- Scan a picture, save it, and import it to Applework Painting, and make changes to it.

Homework # 07
Scanning Pictures
WWW.PAULRALLION.COM

1.- Make a LIST of the steps to scan a picture.
2.- Which picture settings should you use?
3.- Make a LIST of 10 things you can do with a picture after you've scanned it.

Sample Quiz # 07
Scanning Pictures
WWW.PAULRALLION.COM

1.- What do you need to do right before you unplug your USB flash-drive?
2.- What is one thing you can do after you scan a picture?
3.- What is the preferred format to save pictures?
4.- If you want to make changes to the picture, what program could you use?

Handout # 08

Resizing Pictures

WWW.PAULRALLION.COM

Objective: You will learn how to resize a picture file in both Mac and Windows.

Resizing Pictures:

➢ Sometimes picture files are too large to work with, especially when sending them as email attachments. This is how you resize a picture or pictures in both Apple Macs and Windows:

Apple's Preview Program

➢ To resize a picture in Apple's Preview program, select one or more pictures* and click on Tools ⇨ Adjust Size (picture at right). Choose the size you wish to change them to (Small, Medium, Large, or Custom). Preview will show you its resulting size if you choose that option. If you wish to make a copy of the picture, save it with a different name. Otherwise, File ⇨ Save. Apple's Preview has other capabilities: you can rotate a picture, crop it, adjust its colors, etc.

Windows Live Photo Gallery

➢ To resize a picture in Windows Live Photo Gallery, select one or more pictures* and go to Edit ⇨ Resize. Choose the size you wish to change them to: Small, Medium, Large, or Custom. Windows Live Photo Gallery also has many capabilities. You can rotate a picture, crop it, adjust its colors, etc.

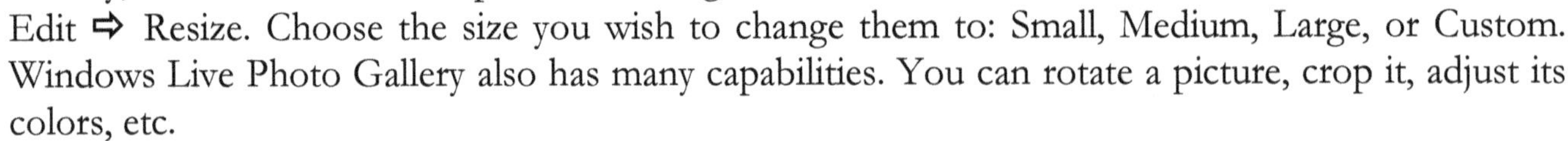

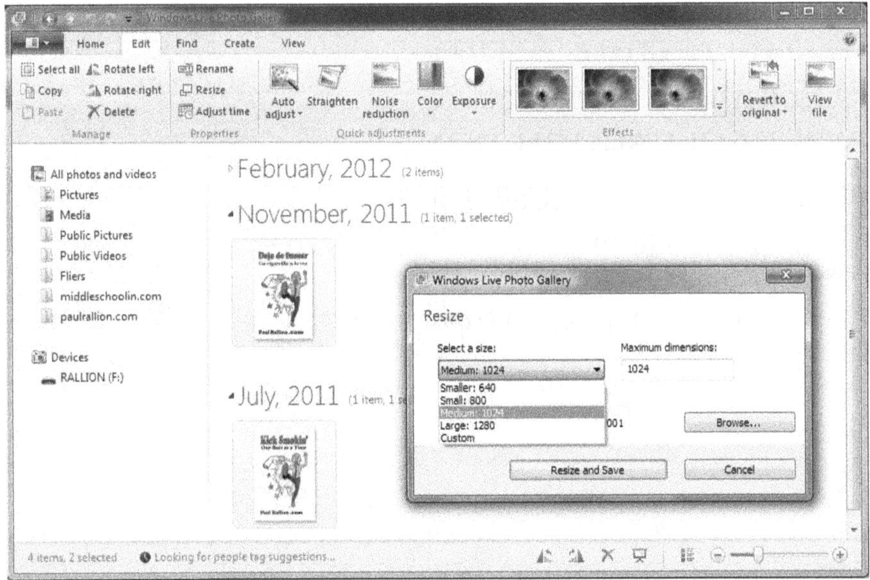

<u>Please note:</u>

Windows Live Photo Gallery needs to import pictures before being able to open them. The good thing is, it does it automatically.

* To select multiple files, click their icons while holding down the Ctrl key (command key in Macs). You can also click on one picture, hold the Shift key and click another picture farther down to select that range of picture files.

Class Project # 08

Resizing Pictures

WWW.PAULRALLION.COM

➢ Find a few pictures on your computer to resize to different sizes, according to either program: Small, Medium, and Large.

Homework # 08

Resizing Pictures

WWW.PAULRALLION.COM

1.- Why would you need to resize a picture?
2.- How do you select multiple files?
3.- How do you resize pictures in Apple's Preview Program?
4.- How do you resize pictures in Windows Live Photo Gallery?

Sample Quiz # 08

Resizing Pictures

WWW.PAULRALLION.COM

1.- What is one thing you can do after you resize a picture?
2.- Which key do you press to select multiple files?
3.- What is Apple's program to resize pictures?
4.- What is Windows' program to resize pictures?

Handout # 09

Preview Program

WWW.PAULRALLION.COM

Objective: In addition to using Apple's Preview program to resize pictures, you will learn how to use more features of Apple's Preview Program.

Change File Formats:

➢ Open your image in Preview and then go to File ⇨ Save As. You have the option of changing the file name, format (.jpg, .gif, .tif, .png, etc.) and adjust its image quality.

Adjust Color:

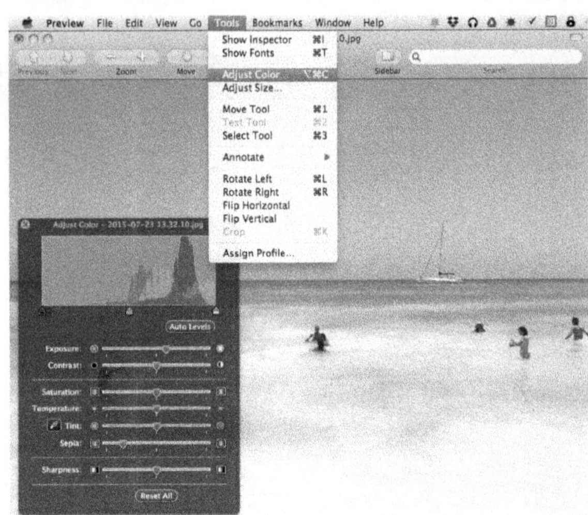

➢ You can adjust the color of pictures (exposure, contrast, saturation, temperature, tint, sepia, and sharpness) by going to Tools ⇨ Adjust Color (picture at right).

Rotate Pictures:

➢ You can go to Tools ⇨ Rotate Left or Right. If you have a trackpad, use a 2-finger gesture to rotate.

Print Preview into PDF Files:

➢ Sometimes it is not necessary to print out a document. To create a PDF version instead, go to File ⇨ Print and click PDF ⇨ Save as PDF.

You can also click on Preview, to open the document in Preview, to see what it'll look on paper.

Annotate Pictures:

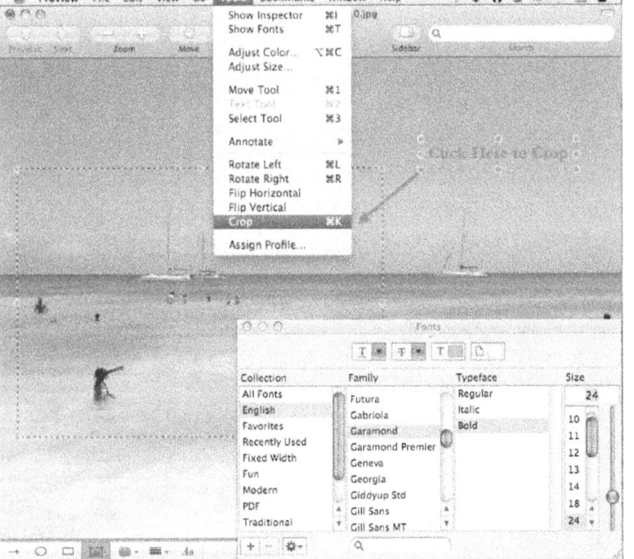

➢ To mark pictures to focus on a specific area, go to Tools ⇨ Annotate ⇨ Add arrows, rectangles, text, etc. by clicking any of the icons that appear on the bottom left corner of the picture at right:

Crop Pictures:

➢ You can crop a picture by clicking the "Select" tool , selecting the part of the picture you wish to keep (adjust if necessary), and click Tools ⇨Crop. You can also press command + K. You can either save your new cropped file, or you can copy/paste it elsewhere.

View a Slideshow:

➢ Select several picture files in Preview using the Finder. Click on a picture file once, hold the Shift key, and press command + O to open all those files in Preview. To view a slideshow, go to View ⇨ Slideshow. Enjoy!

CLASS PROJECT # 09

Preview Program

WWW.PAULRALLION.COM

➢ Scan a picture, save a copy of it, and make some annotations on it. Try to show someone on a picture or point out a detail that may not be so obvious.

HOMEWORK # 09

Preview Program

WWW.PAULRALLION.COM

1.- How do you change a picture's file format?
2.- How do you add annotations to a picture?
3.- How do you crop a picture in Preview?
4.- How do you view a picture slideshow?

SAMPLE QUIZ # 09

Preview Program

WWW.PAULRALLION.COM

1.- In Preview, what is one thing you can change in a picture?
2.- How do you rotate a picture?
3.- Before you can crop a picture, what do you need to do?
4.- Adding markings to a picture is also called:

Apple Finder and Windows Explorer

WWW.PAULRALLION.COM

Objective: You will learn about the Apple's Finder & Windows' Explorer, and their differences.

What are these programs for?

➢ Finder is for Apple, and Explorer is for Windows. Both programs help you keep your files organized, like file cabinets, where you are able to store your documents by placing them in folders. Not only can you name and rename your files and folders, you can sort them by name, by date, by file size, etc. Both of these programs allow you to save your files in pre-named folders: Documents, Music, Downloads, Pictures, etc. Under each folder, you can save files and/or create sub-folders, to keep your files organized. There are different ways to view your files, if you go to the View menu and select: as Icons, as List, as Columns, and as Cover Flow. To create a new folder, go to File ⇨ New Folder.

Apple Finder (top picture at right)

➢ To Rename a file or folder, click its name once, wait one second, and click it again. Another way to do it is to press "Return." When the file/folder name is highlighted, you may rename it. To delete a file or folder, drag it to the trash, or press and hold: "Command" and then press "Delete."

Windows Explorer (bottom picture at right)

➢ To Rename a file or folder, click its name once, wait one second, and click again. However, if you press Return, Windows will open the file! When the file/folder name is highlighted, you may rename it. To delete a file or folder, drag it to the trash, or click on it once, and press "Delete."

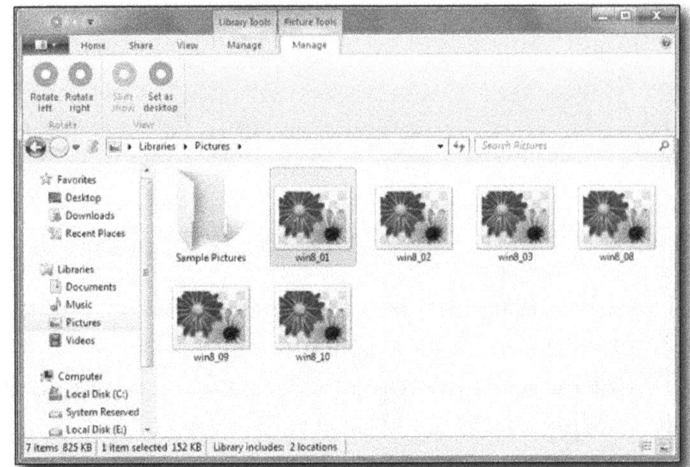

Saving/Naming Files:

➢ When you save your work on most programs, you'll save your work by default as: "untitled." You should give a specific name to your files, otherwise, you may end up with files named: 'untitled 1,' 'untitled 2,' etc. How are you going to know which is which? One suggestion is to save your files starting with the date, for example, if you save your files like this, 202011_Budget.xls, you won't have any trouble knowing the most recent file. Also, do not delete file extensions (.doc, .xls, .ppt, .jpg, etc), they tell the computer what program to opening them with!

CLASS PROJECT # 10
Apple Finder and Windows Explorer
WWW.PAULRALLION.COM

- Practice creating new files and folders, renaming them, and organizing them (drag and drop).

HOMEWORK # 10
Apple Finder and Windows Explorer
WWW.PAULRALLION.COM

1.- What are Explorer and Finder used for?
2.- How do you rename a file/folder in Apple Finder?
3.- How do you rename a file/folder in Windows Explorer?
4.- How should you save your files?

SAMPLE QUIZ # 10
Apple Finder and Windows Explorer
WWW.PAULRALLION.COM

1.- Is Explorer Windows or Mac?
2.- In Windows, what happens if you select and file and press return?
3.- In Mac, what happens if you select and file and press return?
4.- What should you NOT save your files as?

Handout # 11
Photoshop
WWW.PAULRALLION.COM

Objective: You will learn how to perform basic tasks in Photoshop®.

➢ Photoshop® is a popular program used to edit (or modify) graphics, mostly photographs (or pictures). This program is frequently used to adjust a picture's properties (size, cropping, color, brightness, contrast, etc.), or to re-touch pictures (fix red-eye, remove blemishes, etc.) to use on websites, books, magazines, etc.

Other Uses of Photoshop:
Other applications may include altering pictures: adding text to pictures, adding objects to pictures, or changing a picture's background. You can see how the picture (on the right) was made a book cover (below).

Tip: In working with Photoshop®, keep in mind that if you're planning on making major changes to a picture, it is best to first save a copy of the original. That way, you can always start over if you don't like something you did.

Cropping a Picture:
➢ Sometimes a picture contains more things around it than you want. The picture above was cropped from a square to a rectangular picture, below. For example, if you have a picture with an undesired object behind it, or around it, you can just cut it out, or crop it. To crop a picture, click this tool: ⌗, select the part of the picture you wish to keep, adjust if necessary, and press Return. File → Save your new cropped picture!

Adding Text to a Picture:
➢ To add text to a picture, click the Text Tool T, click where you wish to start typing, and type your desired text. If you wish to change the font, size, or color, select the text, and choose your desired setting. Click and drag the text to re-position.

➢ If you make a mistake, always remember a handy tool: Edit → Undo (command + Z), to go back one or more steps.

In the following handouts you'll learn how to do some of the most popular tasks with Photoshop: adjusting a picture's properties, re-touching pictures, and altering pictures. Enjoy!

Class Project # 11
Photoshop
WWW.PAULRALLION.COM

➢ Scan a picture, save a copy of it, and make changes with Photoshop: Crop it and add text to the picture. Have fun!

Homework # 11
Photoshop
WWW.PAULRALLION.COM

1.- What is Photoshop used for?
2.- When learning Photoshop, what's a good tip?
3.- Why do you think a popular use of Photoshop is to work with scanned pictures?
4.- What are other uses of Photoshop?

Sample Quiz # 11
Photoshop
WWW.PAULRALLION.COM

1.- What is a popular use of Photoshop?
2.- Why would you need to re-touch a picture (one example)?
3.- What's a good practice to follow before altering a picture?
4.- If you make a mistake while working on a picture, you can always go back one step:

Handout # 12
Photoshop: Toolbar
WWW.PAULRALLION.COM

Objective: You will learn the tools of Photoshop's toolbar.

Using the Tool Panel (below):

➤ As with other drawing or painting programs, you can find out the name of the tool by slowly hovering your mouse over a tool. From the Photoshop toolbar, you can probably recognize a few tools that are available in other painting programs: Selection tools, cropping tools, brush, text, dropper, mover hand, color palette, etc.
Note: The toolbar shown on the left is the long version of the collapsed toolbar below. Click the toolbar header double arrows to switch between them.

Tips: In working with Photoshop®, keep in mind the following:
➤ If a tool has a small arrow on its bottom right corner, it has more than one tool. Click and hold to see them. You can also press the "control" key prior to clicking on that tool.
➤ If the toolbar is not present, go to Window → Tools. Get other tools by clicking on the same Window menu and selecting: Colors, Layers, Navigator, Options, etc.
➤ You can reposition your toolbar anywhere on the screen by clicking and dragging the tool heading.

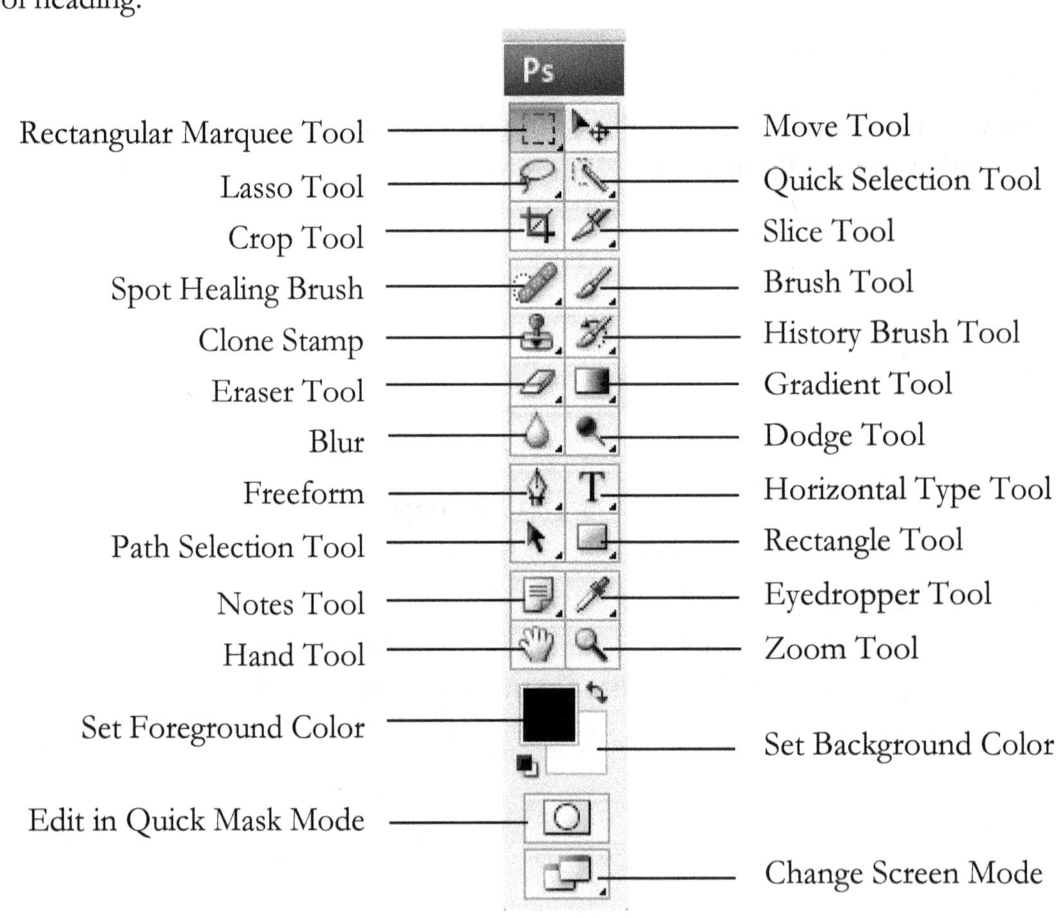

Class Project # 12

Photoshop: Toolbar

WWW.PAULRALLION.COM

➢ Scan a picture, save a copy of it, and make changes with Photoshop. Explore the different tools available. Have fun!

Homework # 12

Photoshop: Toolbar

WWW.PAULRALLION.COM

1.- What are some Photoshop tools that are available in other painting programs?
2.- What does it mean if a tool has a small arrow on its bottom right corner?
3.- What do you do if your tools are not present?
4.- Is the toolbar fixed or can you move around?

Sample Quiz # 12

Photoshop: Toolbar

WWW.PAULRALLION.COM

1.- How can you find out the name of a tool?
2.- If the toolbar is not present, how do you make it appear?
3.- How do you reposition your toolbar?
4.- What does it mean when a tool has a small arrow on its bottom right corner?

HANDOUT # 13

Photoshop: Adjusting Pictures

WWW.PAULRALLION.COM

Objective: You will learn how to adjust a picture in Photoshop®.

➤ Photoshop® is frequently used to adjust a picture's properties (size, cropping, color, brightness, contrast, etc.), to use on websites, magazines, various projects, or just for fun.

Before Adjusting, Altering, or Modifying Pictures:

➤ Before you make changes to a picture, it is best to first save a copy of the original: Go to the Finder, click your file once, and then use Command + "D." You can also open the file in Photoshop and then go to File → Save As, under a different folder and/or name. That way, you can always start over if you don't like something you did.

➤ Another way to protect the original picture is to create "Layers." Think of a layer as a clear sheet of plastic you'll be painting on without affecting the actual picture. To add a layer, go to Layer → New Layer, or click the new layer icon on the bottom right hand side of the screen.

Using Photoshop Filters:

➤ You might want to adjust a picture for various reasons. Photoshop allows you to use several "filters" to change the appearance and 'feel' of the picture. Go to Filter → Filter Gallery, and select from: Artistic, Brush Strokes, Distort, Sketch, Stylize, and Texture. The picture below was adjusted using a filter called: "Ocean Ripple."

- To change a picture's color or brightness, go to Image → Adjustments.
- A useful tool is Filter → Liquify. This tool helps you push pixels around. Try it!

Adjusting Picture Size:

Sometimes a picture is too large to send by email, or to post on a website. While social media sites have the capacity to resize a picture before you post it, other times it is necessary to resize the picture yourself. Go to File → Save for Web & Devices. You can then adjust the quality and image size by clicking on Presets.

Class Project # 13

Photoshop: Adjusting Pictures

WWW.PAULRALLION.COM

➢ Scan a picture, save a copy of it, and make changes with Photoshop: adjust a picture's properties (size, cropping, color, brightness, contrast). Use a Photoshop filter to change the appearance and feel of the picture!

Homework # 13

Photoshop: Adjusting Pictures

WWW.PAULRALLION.COM

1.- How do you make a copy of the original photograph?
2.- What are Layers?
3.- What are some examples of Filters?
4.- How do you resize a picture in Photoshop?

Sample Quiz # 13

Photoshop: Adjusting Pictures

WWW.PAULRALLION.COM

1.- The many ways to change the appearance and feel of pictures is through:
2.- How do you duplicate a picture file in Finder (or Windows Explorer)?
3.- What's one way to protect the original picture?
4.- How do you resize a picture using Photoshop?

HANDOUT # 14

Photoshop: Retouching Pictures

WWW.PAULRALLION.COM

Objective: You will learn how to retouch a picture in Photoshop®.

➢ Photoshop® is frequently used to re-touch pictures (fix red-eye, remove blemishes, restoring old photos, etc.) before being used on websites, books, or other projects.

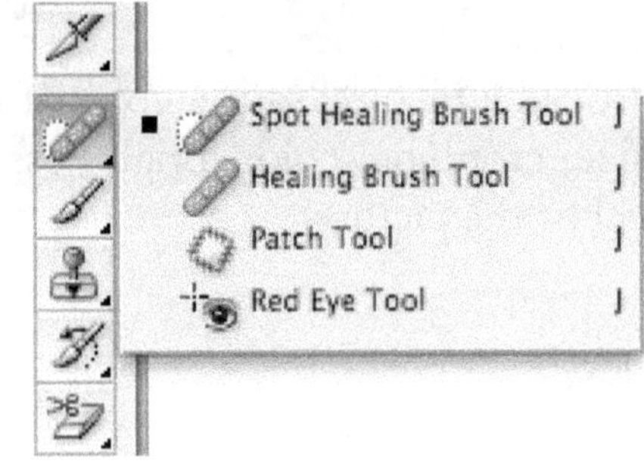

Fixing Red-Eye:

➢ Red-eye is when the eyes of somebody in the picture appear red. This happens when light from the flash bounces from the person's eyes's blood vessels back to the camera. To fix it, click the Red-Eye tool (at right), and then click and drag it over one eye at a time.

Removing Blemishes:

➢ Sometimes a picture contains 'spots' or blemishes. To remove blemishes, use the Spot Healing Brush (at right). Click one spot at a time and let go of your mouse. If you like the change, keep going. Otherwise, go to Edit → Undo (command + Z). If you don't get a circle as a pointer, turn Caps Lock off. Press the "[" key to make the circle smaller, or the "]" key to make it larger.

Restoring Old Photos:

➢ Ask your parents or grandparents if they have an old photograph that you can restore. Scan it (use the handout on scanning pictures) and then open a duplicate of it on Photoshop (or use File → Save As, to save it as a copy with a different name). Below is a picture of my dad. The two instances where the picture was re-touched are: photo paper wrinkle and uniform spots.

Class Project # 14

Photoshop: Retouching Pictures

WWW.PAULRALLION.COM

➢ Ask your parents or grandparents if they have an old photograph that you can restore. Scan it (use the handout on scanning pictures) and then restore it on Photoshop!

Homework # 14

Photoshop: Retouching Pictures

WWW.PAULRALLION.COM

1.- Why does Red-Eye happen?
2.- What other tools are grouped with the Red Eye tool?
3.- How do you remove blemishes?
4.- What are some examples of photo restoration?

Sample Quiz # 14

Photoshop: Retouching Pictures

WWW.PAULRALLION.COM

1.- Name the effect when light bounces off a person's eye's blood vessels.
2.- How do you go back one step?
3.- What's a good practice to follow before altering a picture?
4.- Name one tool that is used to remove "spots."

HANDOUT # 15
Photoshop: Modifying Pictures
WWW.PAULRALLION.COM

Objective: You will learn how to change the background of a picture with Photoshop®.

➢ Photoshop® is frequently used to modify pictures (add or remove objects, modifying its background, etc.) before being used on websites, magazines, various projects, or just for fun!

Changing a picture's background:
➢ Students often ask me how to put a picture of them in a different background. This handout will explain step by step how to achieve that trick. You will need the following:
1) A picture of a person or object that will be in the foreground, and
2) A picture of a different background. Get a picture of a place you'd like to have as a background. How about a picture of one of the wonders of the world, or a picture of the moon surface? Have a picture of yourself, your pet, or an object you'd like to place there. Once you have a duplicate of both pictures (in case you'd like to start over) do the following:
1) Open the picture of the background by going to File → Open. Navigate to the picture you'd like to place in the foreground.
2) Open the picture of the foreground in the same way.
3) Use the Quick Selection Tool and go around the picture you'd like in the foreground. If you select anything extra, hold down your Option key to subtract the unintended selection.
4) Click the Move Tool and drag your selection to the background picture behind it and drop it there. Make sure the background file window shows behind or next to the file window you're selecting yourself from.
5) Drag and position your picture to the desired location on the background.
6) If you need to resize the picture you just placed, go to Edit → Free Transform. Click and drag one of the handles (while holding the Shift key) to resize your picture.
7) Save your work by going to File → Save. You have a few Format options to save your work: a) Photoshop project, which will allow you to make further Photoshop changes, b) Format: JPG, which will allow you to keep a high-resolution picture file, and c) File → Save for Web and Devices, which will let you pick the file type (GIF, JPG, PNG) and let you adjust its size.

➢ If you make a mistake, click on: Edit → Undo, to go back one step.

Class Project # 15

Photoshop: Modifying Pictures

WWW.PAULRALLION.COM

- Get two different pictures: one of yourself and one of different background. Transfer yourself from picture one to picture two.

Homework # 15

Photoshop: Modifying Pictures

WWW.PAULRALLION.COM

1.- What are two things you need to change a picture's background?
2.- What is a good practice before modifying a picture?
3.- How do you resize a picture you just opened in Photoshop?
4.- What do you do immediately after you make a mistake?

Sample Quiz # 15

Photoshop: Modifying Pictures

WWW.PAULRALLION.COM

1.- How many pictures do you need to change a picture's background?
2.- Why would you need to modify a picture (one example)?
3.- What's a good practice to follow before modifying a picture?
4.- What is the tool that will help you to quickly select a person or object?

Handout # 16
Word Processing
WWW.PAULRALLION.COM

Objective: You will learn how to use Microsoft Word® to produce attractive, professional word processing documents. This very handout was produced using a word processor!

What is a word processor for?

➢ You use a word processor to write and format text. For example, to type letters and memos, to create lists, to keep a personal journal, to type your homework, reports, etc.

The Word Processor Window

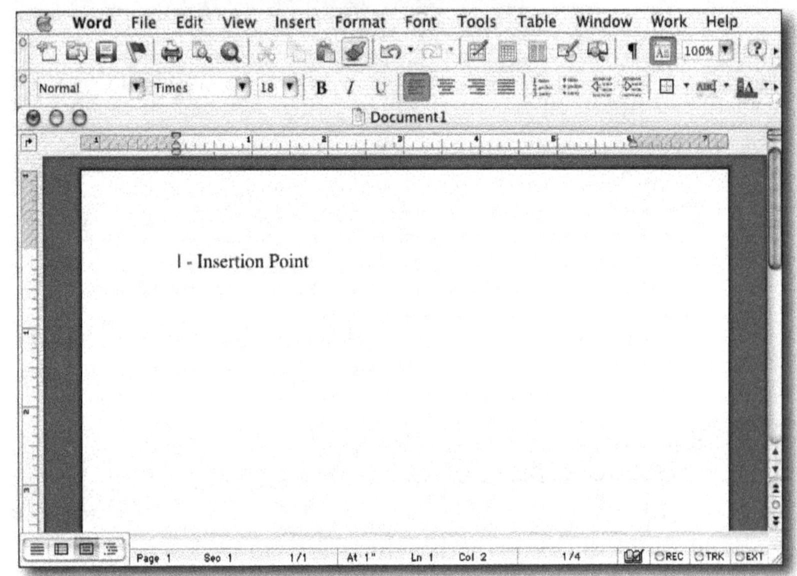

➢ When you open a Microsoft Word® document, you see this window (insert at right). Locate the insertion point (where you can start typing!), the standard toolbar, the formatting toolbar, the margins, and page guides. In general, text in a word processing document looks the same on the screen as it does when printed.

Typing Text

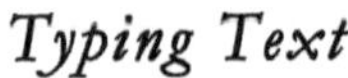

➢ Begin typing text. Do not press Return (or Enter) when you reach the end of the line. The word processor will wrap the words to the next line. You press Return (or Enter) to end a paragraph. Press Return (or Enter) again to insert a blank line. If you wish to delete a character (letter or symbol), place the insertion point to the left of the character and press Delete (in Windows). Press and hold fn and then Delete (in Mac). Place the insertion point to the right of the character and press Delete (in Mac) and Backspace (in Windows).

Aligning Text:

➢ To align text, do not use the space bar! Click somewhere in your text and then select one of the alignment tools on the toolbar. Please refer to the figures below:

Text aligned to the left will have a "misalignment" on the right.	Centered text is mostly used for titles in documents.	Text aligned to the right will have a "misalignment" on the left.	Justified text is aligned on both left and right sides of your document.
Aligned left	**Centered**	**Aligned right**	**Justified**

Class Project # 16
Word Processing
WWW.PAULRALLION.COM

➢ Type a letter, or a one-page report about any topic of your choice. To align text, make sure you use the alignment tools, NOT the space bar.

Homework # 16
Word Processing
WWW.PAULRALLION.COM

1.- What is a word processor for?
2.- When do you need to press "Return"?
3.- Name and draw the alignment tools; what do they do?
4.- What would life be like without word processing?

Sample Quiz # 16
Word Processing
WWW.PAULRALLION.COM

1.- What is the name of the location to start typing?
2.- What do you press to end a paragraph?
3.- What kind of alignment will give you text that is aligned on both sides?
4.- What do you NOT use if you want to align text to the right?

HANDOUT # 17

Word: Selecting Text

WWW.PAULRALLION.COM

Objective: You will learn how to align text using Microsoft Word® to produce attractive, professional word processing documents. This very handout was produced using a word Processor!

SelectingText

➢ Before you can change the appearance of text, you must first highlight (or select it). To highlight text, move the pointer at the beginning of the text you want to select –click and hold your mouse button, and drag to the end of the text –let go. You can also select text using the "Shift" key and the arrow keys. Hold the Shift key and press any arrow key: watch!

Before you can change the appearance of text, you must first highlight (or select it). To highlight text, move the pointer at the beginning of the text you want to select – click and hold your mouse button, and drag to the end of the text –let go. You can also select text using the "Shift" key and the arrow keys. Hold the Shift key and press any arrow key: watch!

Selected Text

After you select your text, you can format it any way you want.

➢ Here are more tips regarding highlighting text:
To highlight a word, click twice on the word.
To highlight a line, place the pointer in the margin and click once.
To highlight a paragraph, place the pointer in the paragraph and click three times.
To highlight everything in a document, go to: *Edit*, and choose: *Select All.*

Line Spacing

➢ To set line spacing, click the decrease-spacing or increase-spacing control on the ruler.

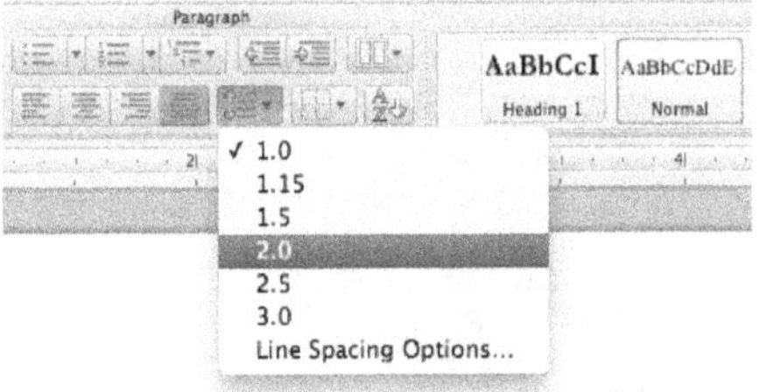

Single-space:
The default line spacing is single space. This setting will not leave any spaces between lines. It will look like this paragraph.

Double-space:

If your teacher asks you to type using double-space, it needs to look like this paragraph. Sometimes teachers make corrections or write comments between the lines of your report.

CLASS PROJECT # 17
Word: Selecting Text
WWW.PAULRALLION.COM

➢ Type a story about a happy event in your life. Include a paragraph where you type it using double-spacing.

HOMEWORK # 17
Word: Selecting Text
WWW.PAULRALLION.COM

1.- How do you select a word, a line, a paragraph?
2.- How do you select everything in a document?
3.- How do you select text using only the keyboard?
4.- Why would a teacher ask you to use double-spacing?

SAMPLE QUIZ # 17
Word: Selecting Text
WWW.PAULRALLION.COM

1.- What is the name of the location to start typing?
2.- A Word Processor is used to write and format:
3.- Before you can change the appearance of text, you must first:
4.- What kind of spacing allows your teacher to write comments about your work?

HANDOUT # 18
Word: Formatting Tools
WWW.PAULRALLION.COM

Objective: You will learn how to format text using Microsoft Word® to produce attractive, professional documents.

Formatting Toolbars:

➢ To make the toolbars appear or disappear, go to the *View* menu, and select *Toolbars*. Make sure that the toolbar you wish to see has a ✓ next to it. To view a description of each icon, place the mouse over it and wait for a description. The first two are the most common toolbars:

Standard Toolbar:

This toolbar contains icons that allow you to open files, save your work, print out your work, preview it, copy, paste, undo, etc., by just clicking once on any of its icons.

Formatting Toolbar:

This toolbar contains icons that allow you to format the text, align it, and even color it, by just clicking once on any of its icons.

Using the Brush

➢ This is probably one of the handiest tools in the Standard Toolbar! The brush allows you to copy the format of text you select from your document and apply it to another text you select so that both have the same format. This is how you use it: Highlight the text you want the format of, click the brush, and then select the text you want to apply the format to. That's all there is to it!

Cut, Copy, Paste

➢ Copy and Paste are probably the most useful tools you will use. Once you have selected the text or the picture you want to copy, you can Cut or Copy it to the Clipboard and Paste it elsewhere in the document (or another document).

To Cut: Go to *Edit*, select *Cut*. The computer removes the selected text, object or image, and places it in the Clipboard.

To Copy: Go to *Edit*, select *Copy*. The computer makes a duplicate of the selected text, object or image. The original item stays in the document and a copy goes to the clipboard.

To Paste: Position the insertion point where you want to place the cut or copied text, object or image, and go to *Edit*, then select *Paste*.

Class Project # 18
Word: Formatting Tools
WWW.PAULRALLION.COM

➢ Type a short report on an interesting topic, format different sections of your work in different ways.

Homework # 18
Word: Formatting Tools
WWW.PAULRALLION.COM

1.- What is the difference between the Standard and the Formatting toolbars?
2.- What can the "Brush" do for you?
3.- What is the difference between Cut and Copy?
4.- What do you use after Cut or Copy?

Sample Quiz # 18
Word: Formatting Tools
WWW.PAULRALLION.COM

1.- How do you make the toolbars appear or disappear?
2.- Which tool bar allows you to format the text, align it, and even color it?
3.- The computer makes a <u>duplicate</u> the selected text, object or image. Cut or Copy?
4.- Name the tool that lets you copy the format of text and apply it to another text

Handout # 19
Word: Formatting Palette
WWW.PAULRALLION.COM

Objective: You will learn how to format text using Microsoft Word's Formatting Palette to produce attractive, professional documents.

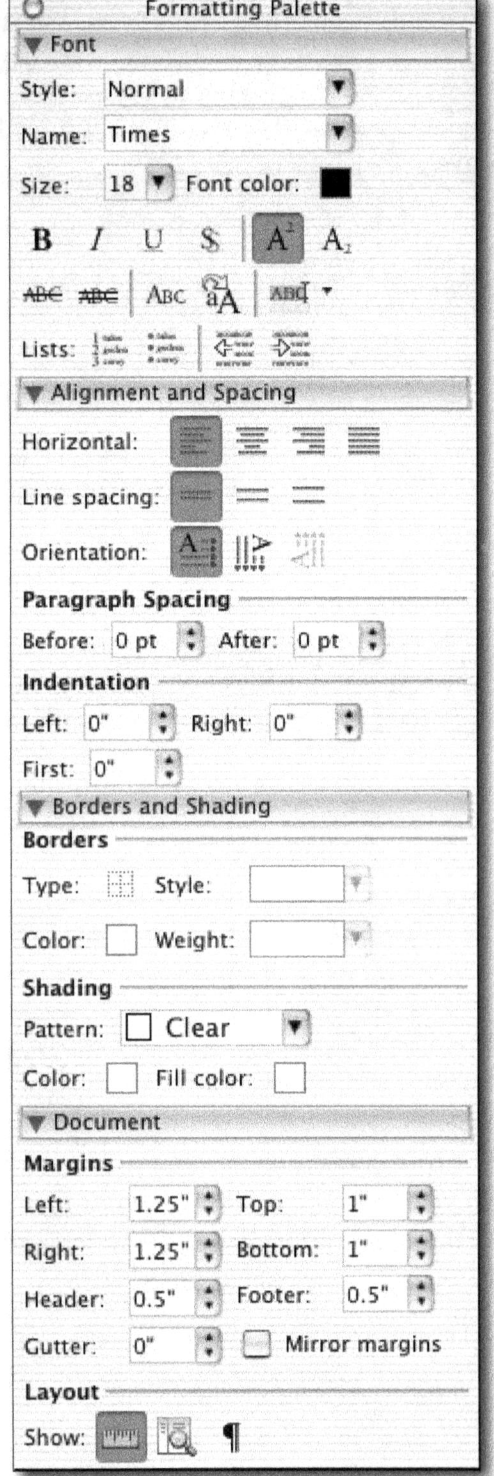

Formatting Palette:

➢ The formatting palette is a handy way to change the appearance of your document! To make the formatting palette appear, go to the *View* menu and select: *Formatting Palette.*

➢ You can format the Font, the Alignment and Spacing, the Borders and Shading, and the Document itself. First you need to click these headings to expand those menus.

➢ You can either select the format first and then type, or you can type first and then change the format. If you type first and then want to change the format, you need to select or highlight the text you want to format and then use the formatting palette to make any changes (insert at right). The best way to learn the formatting palette is to explore the options yourself!

Changing Your Mind

➢ If you make a mistake or change your mind after you have made a change, you can undo the last change, or go back to the last saved version of your document.

To Undo: Go to *Edit*, select *Undo*. This will undo the last step.

To Revert: That is, to remove all the changes you have made since the last saved document, go to *File*, select *Revert*. Another way you can do this is to close the file without saving changes, and then opening the file again.

It Doesn't Fit

➢ Sometimes you may need a one-page report but end up with two pages, the second page containing one or two lines. To avoid this, reduce the size of the font, or change the font type to fit the text in one page. You can also reduce the margins. Click on "Document" and reduce the margin sizes.

Note: To avoid printing out a blank page at the end of your document, delete the space below your last line. The best way to do this is to click after your last character and use the right-delete key delete. This key will erase text to the right of the cursor. If you have a laptop keyboard, press and hold the "Function" key (Fn), and then press and hold the Delete key.

Class Project # 19
Word: Formatting Palette
WWW.PAULRALLION.COM

➢ Type a short report on an interesting topic, format different sections of your work in different ways using the formatting palette.

Homework # 19
Word: Formatting Palette
WWW.PAULRALLION.COM

1.- What is the main function of the formatting palette?
2.- How do you expand the menus?
3.- Should you type first and then format, or first format and then type?
4.- What is the difference between Undo and Revert?

Sample Quiz # 19
Word: Formatting Palette
WWW.PAULRALLION.COM

1.- How do you get the Formatting Palette to show?
2.- What kind of alignment tool do you use to type your name, period #, and the date?
3.- How do you expand the menus?
4.- How do you go back one step in your work?

Handout # 20
Word: Adding Pictures to Text
WWW.PAULRALLION.COM

Objective: You will learn how to add a picture to a text document, and how to wrap a picture with text using Microsoft Word®.

Adding Pictures To Text

➢ You can add pictures to text (such as clip art, your drawings, or pictures!) so they move along with your text. The main advantage of text-wrapping is that by saving space in your document, you can save paper as well. It also looks more decorative, more professional.

Adding Pictures To Move Along With Text

➢ To add a picture to your document go to Insert – Picture from either Clip Art® or From File. Another way to add a picture is to select (or highlight) the picture and go to the *Edit* menu and choose "*Copy*" from your painting program. Place the insertion point in the text, and then go to the *Edit* menu and choose "*Paste.*"

The picture will look like this with respect to the rest of the text.

Adding Pictures So That Text Wraps Them

➢ To add a picture so that the text wraps it, go to Insert ⇨ Picture from either Clip Art® or From File. Another way to insert a picture is to go to a drawing or painting program and go to *Edit* and choose "*Copy.*" Now go back to the word processor file and go to the *Edit* menu and choose "*Paste.*" Double-click on the picture, click on the "Layout" Tab, and select "Tight." The picture will look like this with respect to the rest of the text.

Are there different kinds of Text Wrap?

➢ Yes, there is regular, or square text wrap, and there is irregular, or tight text wrap.

- Irregular or Tight Text Wrap will wrap the text according to the shape of the image. Please refer to the picture from the previous paragraph.
- Regular or Square Text Wrap will wrap the text around an imaginary "square" formed by the picture. In this case you would double-click on the picture, click on the "Layout" Tab, and select "Square." Compare the last two text-wrapped pictures of a computer. Can you tell the difference in text-wrapping?

Class Project # 20

Word: Adding Pictures to Text

WWW.PAULRALLION.COM

- Type your own autobiography. Type one page and add your own picture taken with a digital camera. Make sure your picture is square text-wrapped.

Homework # 20

Word: Adding Pictures to Text

WWW.PAULRALLION.COM

1.- What is the difference between Square Text-Wrap and Tight Text-Wrap?
2.- How is Text Wrapping useful? (Give 2 reasons)

Sample Quiz # 20

Word: Adding Pictures to Text

WWW.PAULRALLION.COM

1.- What is the easiest way to insert a picture into a Word document?
2.- When you double click the picture, which tab do you select for picture text-wrapping?
3.- What kind of text wrap will write text according to an imaginary box?
4.- What kind of text wrap will write text according to the shape of the image?

HANDOUT # 21
Word: Making A Flyer
WWW.PAULRALLION.COM

Objective: You will learn how to make a flyer using Microsoft Word®.

Word Document Gallery:
➢ You can choose a Flyer Template from Microsoft Word, one that's already done. All you have to do is replace the text with yours. To select a Template, go to File → New From Template, and click on "Flyers" on the left column. You can do the same for Newsletters, Brochures, Certificates, etc.

Adding Word Art:
➢ To add some fancy text, go to Insert → WordArt. Click one of the styles below:

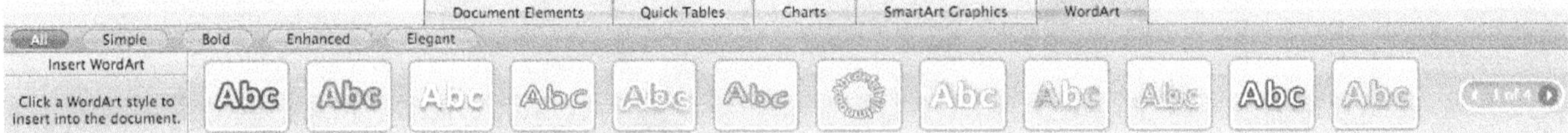

This kind of text will appear: **Your Text Here** Double-click the text to change its format.

Page Border:
➢ To add a border to your flyer, go to Format → Borders and Shading. Click on Page Border, and choose from: Box, Shadow, 3-D, or Custom. You can also select Style, Color, Width, and Art.

Page Background:
➢ You can add a color to your background, a picture background, or a watermark. A watermark is a very light version of print on thc page. To change your page's background color, go to Format → Background, and select a color. Do not close that window; click on "Fill Effects." You can change: Gradient, Texture, Pattern, Picture. To place a picture on the background, click Picture → Select Picture.

Coupons or Tear-offs:
➢ You can add a coupon and a row of tear-offs on the bottom of your flyer by using the "Text Box." Go to Insert → Text Box. Click and drag on the page how big you wish your text box. Then, type in it. In order to draw the dotted lines on the text box, we need to add a border. Cross-click (press control while clicking) on the border of your text box, and select "Format Text Box." Under "Line," click the dropdown menu: Color, and select your favorite color. Under Color, select "Dashed." Click OK!

Enjoy your flyer!

Class Project # 21
Word: Making A Flyer
WWW.PAULRALLION.COM

➢ Make a flyer for an event you may have coming up: a party, a yard sale, etc. Don't have an event coming up? Make one up!

Homework # 21
Word: Making A Flyer
WWW.PAULRALLION.COM

1.- How do you get a template from MS Word for a new flyer?
2.- Why would you want to add a border to your flyer?
3.- What is a page watermark?
4.- What is the purpose of having tear-offs on the bottom of a flyer?

Sample Quiz # 21
Word: Making A Flyer
WWW.PAULRALLION.COM

1.- Fancy text that can be added and modified is called:
2.- To add a border you go to Format, and then?
3.- A very light version of print on the page to make it more unique is called:
4.- Coupons and tear-offs are made by using:

Handout # 22
Word: Header and Footer
WWW.PAULRALLION.COM

Objective: You will learn how to use Header and Footer using Microsoft Word®.

Header and Footes:

➢ Sometimes students click on the white area at the top of the page (in Print Layout View, the default view), without realizing they have entered the Header of the page. They are later surprised to find out that what they type there appears on all the pages of their report! However, that could be a good thing, if you know how to use them. The most common use of this feature is to number the pages of a report.

Page Numbering:

➢ To access the Headers and Footers, go to View > Header and Footer. Click the Header and Footer bar next to "Home" to show the menu below:

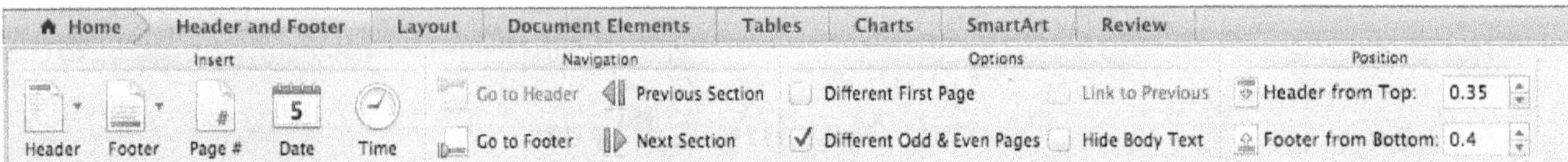

To insert page numbers on the bottom of each page, click on "Go to Footer" and click on "Page #." The program will place a 1 in the footer. You can use the alignment tools to center the page numbers and also to change the font, size, style, etc.

Advanced Uses of Header and Footer:

➢ An example of multiple Header and Footer functions is illustrated below:

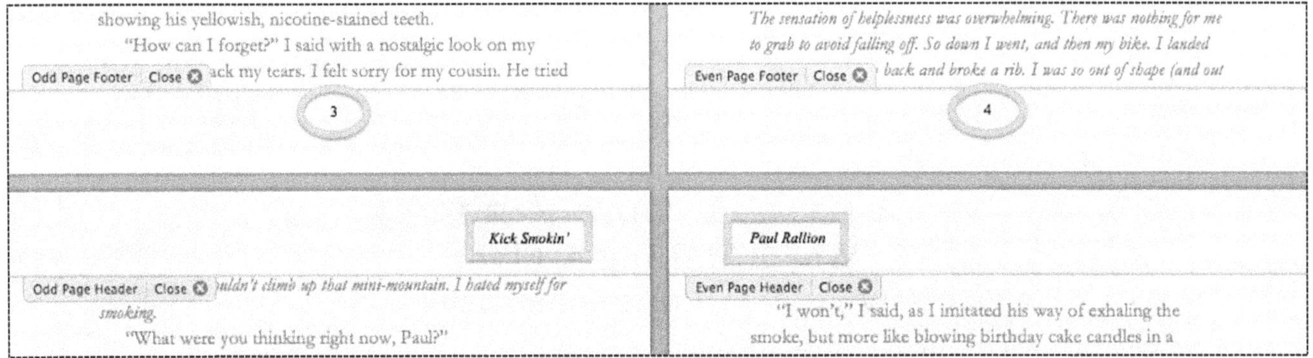

- The first quadrant represents Odd Page Footer with odd number pages.
- The second quadrant represents Even Page Footer, with even number pages –ovals show page numbers.
- The third quadrant represents Odd Page Header with the book title: *Kick Smokin'*.
- The fourth quadrant represents Even Page Header with the author name: *Paul Rallion* –rectangles show headers.

Class Project # 22
Word: Header and Footer
WWW.PAULRALLION.COM

➢ Type a report of a pages, and number the pages of the report by using footer tools. Center the page numbers and use a fancy font.

Homework # 22
Word: Header and Footer
WWW.PAULRALLION.COM

1.- What are header and footer?
2.- How do you access the header and footer?
3.- How do you format the header and footer?
4.- Give an example of an advanced use of header and footer.

Sample Quiz # 22
Word: Header and Footer
WWW.PAULRALLION.COM

1.- What's the most common use of headers and footers?
2.- How do you access the header and footer?
3.- The Header and Footer can be formatted: True or False?
4.- The Header and Footer usually appear on every page of your docuemnt: True or False?

HANDOUT # 23
Simple Text
WWW.PAULRALLION.COM

Objective: You will learn how to use a simple text program.

What are TextEdit or WordPad for?

➢ TextEdit and WordPad are simple text programs that are used to write a quick text file that does not require fancy formatting, like you would with a full word processing program. For example, you can type a quick line, memos, short lists, keep a journal, type your homework, etc. You can also use these simple text programs to write code (programming). Some of the advantages of TextEdit and WordPad are how quickly they launch and the little memory they require to run.

The TextEdit and WordPad Window:

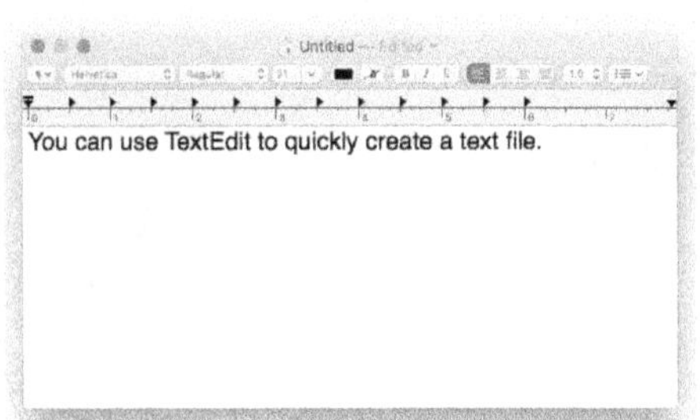

➢ When you open a TextEdit document, you see this window (insert at right). Like in a word processor, do not press Return (or Enter) when you reach the end of the line. The program will wrap the words to the next line. Press Return (or Enter) to end a paragraph. Press Return (or Enter) again to insert a blank line.

Removing Text Format:

➢ Has it happened to you that you paste a certain amount of text onto your world processing document, but it's formatted differently than your work? Sometimes you need to remove all formatting from a text before pasting it. The way to do that is, paste that format-rich text onto a Text Edit document and then go to Format > Make Plain Text. As you can see below, the window on the left has text formatted in different colors and it is highlighted. The window on the right has the same text with all the formatting removed:

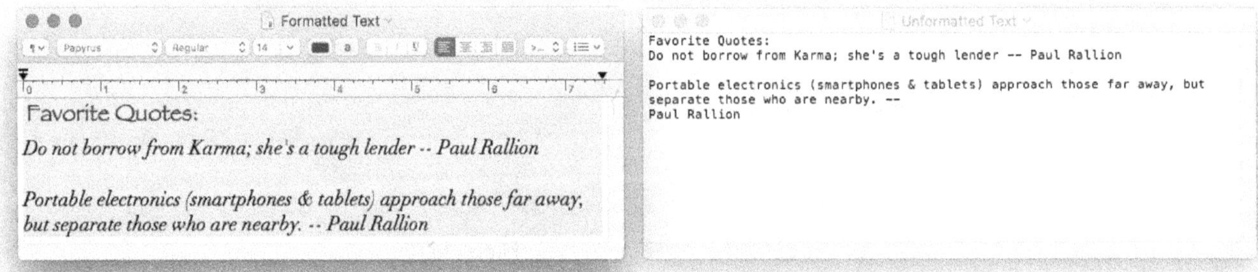

Programming:

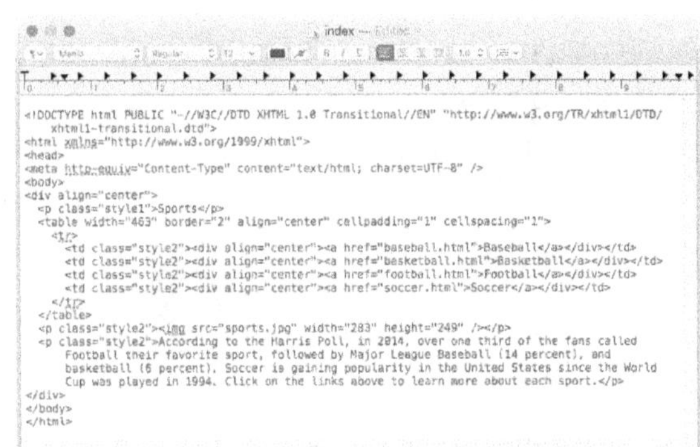

➢ Other uses of SimpleText and WordPad include programming, where lines of commands (or code) are used to write and/or edit programs. To open a file in SimpeText or WordPad, go to its icon (Finder or Explorer), cross-click (or hold the Ctrl key and then click), and select: Open With: TextEdit or WordPad.

Class Project # 23
Simple Text
WWW.PAULRALLION.COM

- Create a quick text edit file, take notes on the next class, and save it.

Homework # 23
Simple Text
WWW.PAULRALLION.COM

1.- What is a Simple Text?
2.- When do you need to press "Return"?
3.- How do you remove the format from text?
4.- How do you open a file in Simple Text?

Sample Quiz # 23
Simple Text
WWW.PAULRALLION.COM

1.- What is one example of a Simple Text program?
2.- Name one instance when you need to press Return:
3.- Before pasting text, it is sometimes a good idea to:
4.- What is one important use of a Simple Text program?

Handout # 24
Introduction to Spreadsheet
WWW.PAULRALLION.COM

Objective: You will learn what a Spreadsheet is and some of its applications.

What is a Spreadsheet?

➢ A spreadsheet is an arrangement of rows and columns of cells used to enter, calculate, organize, and analyze information. Spreadsheets are used to prepare budgets, financial statements, inventory management, and calculate projections. Refer to the picture at right. Rows are identified by numbers, and columns are identified by letters of the alphabet. Can you find the rows and columns? There are more than 26 columns, but there are only 26 letters in the alphabet. How do you think they labeled them after column "Z"?

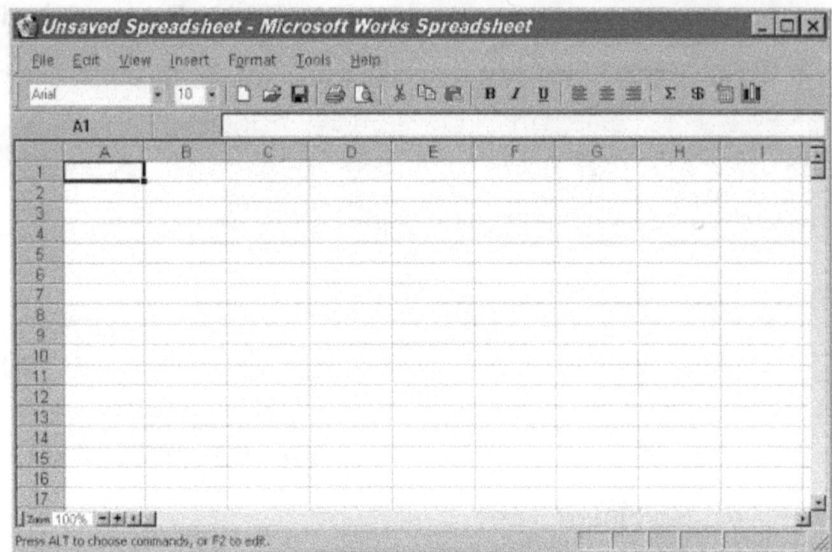

What is a Cell?

➢ A cell is the point where a column and a row intersect. This intersection or cell has a name that is given by the column letter and the row number. For example, the first cell in a worksheet is cell A1 (column A, row 1). The **active cell** is the cell in which you are currently working. It will have a darker border around it. In the picture above, the active cell happens to be A1.

Entering Data into a Spreadsheet

➢ There are three types of data found on a spreadsheet: A **label**, which is letters; a **value**, which is a number; and a **formula**, which is a statement that performs a calculation.

Moving Around in a Spreadsheet

➢ The first thing you need to do to enter or edit data into a cell, you need to select it to make it active. You can use the mouse or the arrows (up, down, left, right) on the keyboard. You can also use **PgUp** and **PgDn** to move the active cell up or down one full screen. Press the **Home** key, and move the active cell to Column A of the current row. Lastly, **Ctrl + Home** will move the active cell to cell A1.

CLASS PROJECT # 24
Introduction to Spreadsheet
WWW.PAULRALLION.COM

➢ In Spreadsheet, make a table of anything to get you familiarized with Spreadsheet: Your class schedule, your weekly allowances, or the number of hours you study at home for each subject, a list of friends with their date of birth, favorite color, song, etc.

HOMEWORK # 24
Introduction to Spreadsheet
WWW.PAULRALLION.COM

1.- What is a spreadsheet?
2.- Give two more examples of what spreadsheets are used for.
3.- How are cells identified?
4.- What's the name of the 27th spreadsheet column?

SAMPLE QUIZ # 24
Introduction to Spreadsheet
WWW.PAULRALLION.COM

1.- A spreadsheet is an arrangement of rows and:
2.- Name one thing spreadsheets are used for:
3.- The point where a row and a (answer for #1) intersect is called:
4.- Three types of data can be entered into a spreadsheet: A label, a value, and a:

HANDOUT # 25

Excel: Formatting a Spreadsheet

WWW.PAULRALLION.COM

Objective: You will learn how to format a Spreadsheet.

Resizing Columns and Rows

➤ To resize a column (or a row), place your mouse pointer on the right edge of the column heading (or on the bottom of the row heading) you want to resize, until your arrow becomes a double line with a double arrow. Look for the word *Resize* on the picture at right. Then click and hold your mouse button, and slide left or right (for columns), and up or down (for rows). Let go.

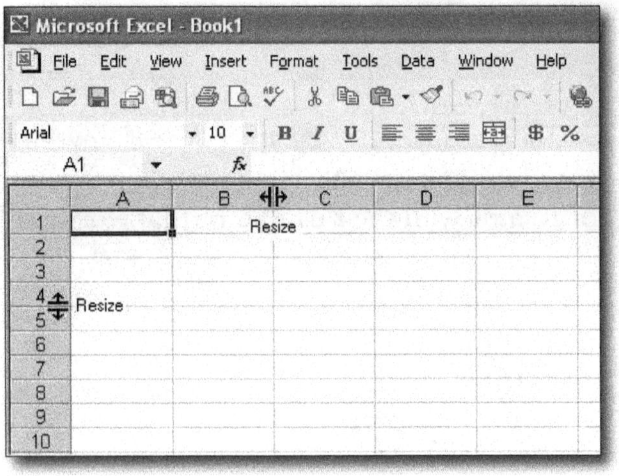

Selecting Cells and Ranges

➤ Before you can change, format, enter, or work with data you must select a cell or a cell range (a group of adjacent cells). Here is how:

To select one cell:	Click the cell.
To select a cell range:	Hold down the mouse button and drag the pointer over the cells you want to select.
To select an entire row or column:	Click the row or column heading.
To select the entire spreadsheet:	Click the blank button to the left of the A (column A) and above the 1 (row 1). Or, go to *Edit* and choose *Select All.*

Moving, Copying and Deleting Data

➤ You Cut, Copy, and Paste data in spreadsheet the same way you do in Painting, Drawing, or Word Processor. Go to: *Edit,* select *Copy.* Then go to *Edit*, and select *Paste.*

Formatting Cell Data

➤ You can change the format of any part of your spreadsheet. Start by selecting the text, cell, cell range, column, or row that you want to change. Then go to *Format* and select *Cells.* From the window, select the tab you wish: *Number, Alignment, Font, Border, etc.*

Adding Borders, Colors to Cells

➤ Select the cells, go to *Format,* and select *Cells.* Then select the *Border* tab.

Inserting or Deleting Rows and Columns

➤ Select one or more rows or columns by clicking their heading. To insert, go to *Insert,* and then choose *Row* or *Column.* To delete, go to *Edit* and select *Delete.*

Class Project # 25

Excel: Formatting a Spreadsheet

WWW.PAULRALLION.COM

➢ Use the table that you made from the previous handout, or make a new one. Format its text color, type, size, resize cells, add borders, etc.

Homework # 25

Excel: Formatting a Spreadsheet

WWW.PAULRALLION.COM

1.- How do you resize a column or a row?
2.- How do you select an entire row or column?
3.- How do you add borders and colors to cells?
4.- How do you insert or delete a row or column?

Sample Quiz # 25

Excel: Formatting a Spreadsheet

WWW.PAULRALLION.COM

1.- What do you do to select one cell?
2.- To resize a row or column you place your pointer until it becomes a:
3.- To select an entire row or an entire column, you click the row's or column's _______.
4.- To select the whole spreadsheet you click the button that touches column A and row:

HANDOUT # 26

Excel: Math

WWW.PAULRALLION.COM

Objective: You will learn how to use a Spreadsheet for mathematical purposes.

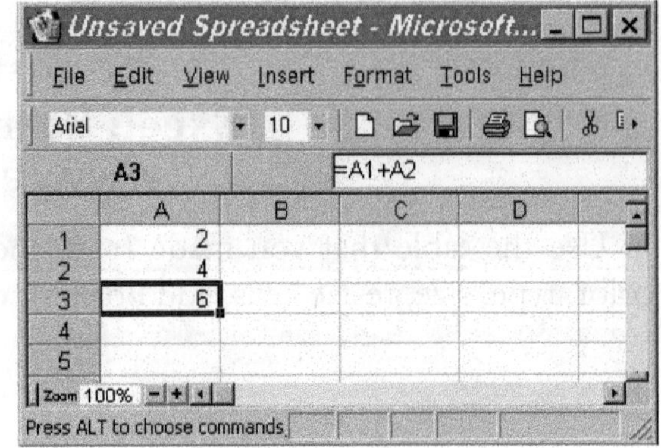

Working with Formulas

➢ Formulas can be simple and complicated. ALL formulas start with an equal sign (=). Spreadsheet will show the number value on the cell, and the formula on the formula bar (please refer to insert at right).

Here are a few examples of simple formulas:

=A7+C9	Adds the values in cells A7 and C9.
=C2*7.5	Multiplies the value in cell C2 by 7.5, a number that was typed.
=SUM(C2..C7)	Uses the SUM function to add the values in the cell range C2 to C7.

Entering Numbers and Formulas

➢ To enter a number or a formula, say, to add 2 plus 4 equals 6, do this: click in cell A1. Type the number 2. Then click in A2 and type the number 4. Then click in A3 (where you want the answer) and type the formula =A1+A2 and then Return (or Enter). That's it!

Try Some:

➢ Now do these additions (+) using Spreadsheet:

2	11	34	56	95	29	54	38	28	17	95	53
+ 4	+ 25	+ 17	+ 37	+ 18	+ 72	+ 71	+ 29	+ 15	+ 39	+ 11	+ 80

Using the same numbers, have Spreadsheet perform subtractions (-), multiplications (*), and divisions (/).

Errors messages in Spreadsheet

➢ Once in a while you may get an error message. Error messages start with the number sign (#) and end with an exclamation point (!). Here they are:

#######	The column is too narrow. Resize it by making it wider.
#DIV/0!	Dividing a number by zero is not allowed.
#VALUE!	Check that the reference is a number value, not text.
#REF!	Wrong reference number. Check your formula.

Class Project # 26

Excel: Math

WWW.PAULRALLION.COM

➢ Perform the Additions (+), Subtractions (-), Multiplications (*), and Divisions (/) with the same numbers from the handout under the section ***Try Some***. Use a different *Sheet* for each one.

Homework # 26

Excel: Math

WWW.PAULRALLION.COM

1.- What do ALL formulas start with?
2.- Write a short formula to add ALL the numbers from cell D5 to D29:
3.- What do you do if you get this: #####
4.- Which cell do you type the formula in?

Sample Quiz # 26

Excel: Math

WWW.PAULRALLION.COM

1.- All formulas start with:
2.- Write the formula to add A7 plus C9:
3.- What do you need to do if your column shows this: #######.
4.- How do you select ALL cells on your worksheet?

HANDOUT # 27

Excel: Saving Money

WWW.PAULRALLION.COM

Objective: You will learn how to use a Spreadsheet to manage money, specifically, to calculate how money "grows" when invested.

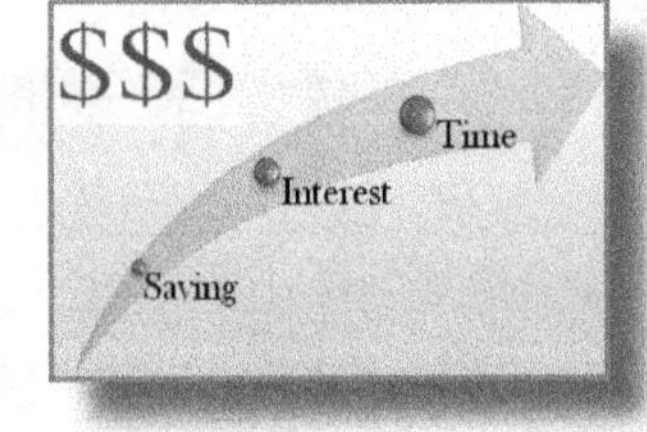

Money Management in Middle School

➢ Money is not a topic offered in every school, although some experts say it should be. Students your age may not have a lot of money, but what you do have on your side is *time*. So, the key for you to start accumulating money is to combine three ingredients: Saving + Interest + Time…

Budget

➢ You may be familiar with 'budgeting' if you have planned on saving or spending any money. For example, if you receive an allowance from your parents, you decide how to spend and save your money. You can either buy a pack of gum, or save your money.

How to Calculate Your Life Savings!

➢ Try this. Suppose you save $10 per month, and at the beginning of the following year you deposit $120 into a 1-year CD (not a compact disc, but Certificate of Deposit) earning 5% interest. Using a spreadsheet program like Microsoft Excel or Google Spreadsheet, set up a table like this:

	A	B	C	D	E	F	G	H
1	Year	2010	2011	2012	2013	2014	2015	2016
2	Deposit	$120.00	$120.00	$120.00	$120.00	$120.00	$120.00	$120.00
3	Prev. Balance	$0.00	$126.00	$258.30	$397.22	$543.08	$696.23	$857.04
4	Interest	$6.00	$12.30	$18.92	$25.86	$33.15	$40.81	$48.85
5	Balance	$126.00	$258.30	$397.22	$543.08	$696.23	$857.04	$1,025.89

Type the headings above and to the left (Year, Deposit, Previous Balance, etc.) and enter $120 in cell B2. Since this is a new account, enter $0 in cell B3 (previous balance in 2010 is $0). Your 5% interest is calculated as: *=(B2+B3)*5%* (enter this formula in cell B4). You then get your balance for 2010 by adding the numbers: *=B2+B3+B4* (type this formula in cell B5). For 2011 you repeat the process except that for "Previous Balance," you type *=B5* in cell C3. Try this for 10, 20, or 30 years and see how much money you end up with just by saving $10 per month!

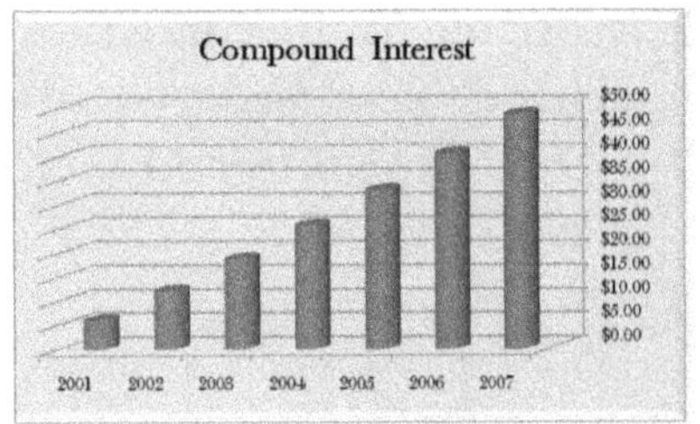

You have "time and interest" on your side. The chart on the right shows you how *compound interest* works: the interest you earn is added to the principal and earns interest as well. From the chart on the right, notice how the interest is slightly higher every time. How much money then, would you need to save yearly, in order to have $1 million in 30 years?

Class Project # 27

Excel: Saving Money

WWW.PAULRALLION.COM

➢ Work out a schedule to find out how much interest $120 (which is just $10/month) would earn at 5% in 10, 20, and 30 years.

Homework # 27

Excel: Saving Money

WWW.PAULRALLION.COM

1.- What is the most important factor in saving money for your future?
2.- What are five things you can do to save more money?
3.- Look up the definition of the word: budget.
4.- What is compound interest?

Sample Quiz # 27

Excel: Saving Money

WWW.PAULRALLION.COM

1.- Interest that earns interest is called:
2.- To find how much B2 would earn at 7% interest, the formula would be:
3.- What do you need to do if your column shows this: ######.
4.- To select an entire row or an entire column, you click the row's or column's _______.

HANDOUT # 28

Excel: Credit Repayment

WWW.PAULRALLION.COM

Objective: You will learn how to use a Spreadsheet to manage money, specifically, the cost of repaying a loan, i.e; credit card, student loan, personal loan, etc.

Money Management in Middle School

➢ Just like saving money (previous handout) is rewarded when you start early, it is also important to learn early that credit is like "renting money." More specifically, when you borrow money you pay interest on it, sort of like: "rent." Usually the highest interest is paid on credit card debt, especially credit cards at department stores (18%, 21%, or even 25%+). Be careful also with 'teaser rates,' which usually last only a few months, and then reset to higher interest rates.

Credit Repayment

➢ Try this. Suppose you owe $1,000.00 at 15% interest and you wish to pay $50.00 per month (perhaps the minimum required payment is only $20 but you want to pay more). Using a spreadsheet program like Microsoft Excel or Google Spreadsheet, set up a table like this:

	A	B	C	D	E	F	G	H	I	J	K	L	M
1	2010	Jan	Feb	March	April	May	June	July	Aug	Sept	Oct	Nov	Dec
2	Credit	$1,000.00	$962.50	$924.53	$886.09	$847.16	$807.75	$767.85	$727.45	$686.54	$645.12	$603.19	$560.73
3	Interest	$12.50	$12.03	$11.56	$11.08	$10.59	$10.10	$9.60	$9.09	$8.58	$8.06	$7.54	$7.01
4	Payment	$50.00	$50.00	$50.00	$50.00	$50.00	$50.00	$50.00	$50.00	$50.00	$50.00	$50.00	$50.00
5	Balance	$962.50	$924.53	$886.09	$847.16	$807.75	$767.85	$727.45	$686.54	$645.12	$603.19	$560.73	$517.74

Type the headings above and to the left (Months, Credit, Interest, Payment, & Balance) and enter $1000 in cell B2. Your interest is calculated as: *=B2*15%/12* (12 months in a year). Type this formula in cell B3 Enter your payment in cell B4 as $50. You then get your balance for January 2010 by typing this formula: *=B2+B3-B4*. Start Feb 2010 with the amount you ended in Jan 2010, so type =B5 in cell C2. Continue calculating the interest and balance this way for the rest of 2010.

For the following year, 2011, skip row 6, and type the same headings above and to the left. Cell A7 (2011), cell A8 (Credit), etc. In cell B8 your previous balance is the amount of Dec 2010, or $517.74, so type =M5. Continue in 2011 the same way you did in 2010 until your balance is paid in full, or zero. *Hint:* Your last payment is not $50. Notice that in interest alone you paid $117.74 in 2010.

Of course, the best way to use credit cards it to pay the balance in full each month. So, what's better, saving for something and earning interest, or paying interest on something you're buying on credit?

Tip: To complete a series in Spreadsheet, select two cells (January and February), click and hold the bottom right-hand corner of the second selected cell and drag to the right. Watch what happens!

Class Project # 28

Excel: Credit Repayment

WWW.PAULRALLION.COM

➢ Work out a schedule to repay $1,000.00 at 15% with a monthly payment of $50.00. How long will it take you to pay off the debt?

Homework # 28

Excel: Credit Repayment

WWW.PAULRALLION.COM

1.- Where do banks get the money to pay those who save?
2.- What kind of credit costs the most?
3.- What is the best way to use a credit card?
4.- Why is it better to save for something than to buy on credit?

Sample Quiz # 28

Excel: Credit Repayment

WWW.PAULRALLION.COM

1.- How many cells do you need to drag from, to complete a series?
2.- The formula to find out how much interest B2 would pay at 18% in one month would be:
3.- Why do you need to divide credit formula by 12?
4.- What's the best way to use a credit card?

HANDOUT # 29

Excel: Graphs and Charts

WWW.PAULRALLION.COM

Objective: You will learn how to use a Spreadsheet to make Charts.

Making Charts

➢ To make a chart, select a range of cells from a table and then go to the *Insert* menu and select *Chart.* In the Chart Options dialog box, click a chart type in the Gallery, and then click next as you go. Spreadsheet draws the chart and places it on top of the spreadsheet. The default title is the data in the upper-left cell in the selected range.

Bar Graphs

➢ A **bar graph** uses bars (either vertical or horizontal) to display amounts in the spreadsheet. In the bar chart illustration, the **Y axis**, or vertical scale, displays the values from the table, which range from 0 to 10 million. The **X axis**, or horizontal scale, displays the labels or names of the schools. The legend below the chart identifies the data being charted through the use of color or shading. You can see in this chart the car production by 5 manufacturers over 3 years.

MOTOR VEHICLE PRODUCTION			
	2008	2009	2010
Toyota	9,237,780	7,234,439	8,557,351
GM	8,282,803	6,459,053	8,476,192
VW	6,517,288	6,054,829	7,341,065
Hyundai	2,777,137	4,645,776	5,764,918
Ford	5,407,000	4,685,394	4,988,031

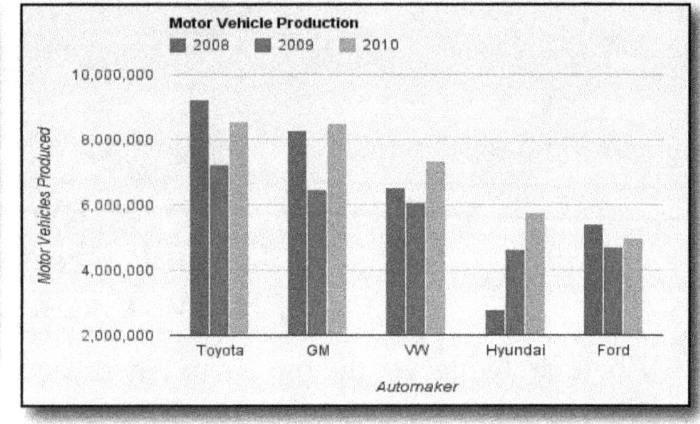

Pie Charts

➢ A **pie chart** takes the form of a circle divided into pieces or slices to visually show the relationship of data in a spreadsheet. Each slice represents one of the values in the spreadsheet. The whole circle represents the total of all the amounts. Pie charts are especially appropriate for displaying percentages of a whole, and the software will automatically calculate the percentages. In the illustration, each slice of the chart represents a percentage of the total population. The labels and percentages make it easy to see which are the most populated continents.

2011 WORLD POPULATION	
Asia	4,140,336,501
Africa	994,527,534
Europe	738,523,843
N. America	528,720,588
S. America	385,742,554
Oceania	36,102,071
Antartica	4,490
Total	6,823,957,581

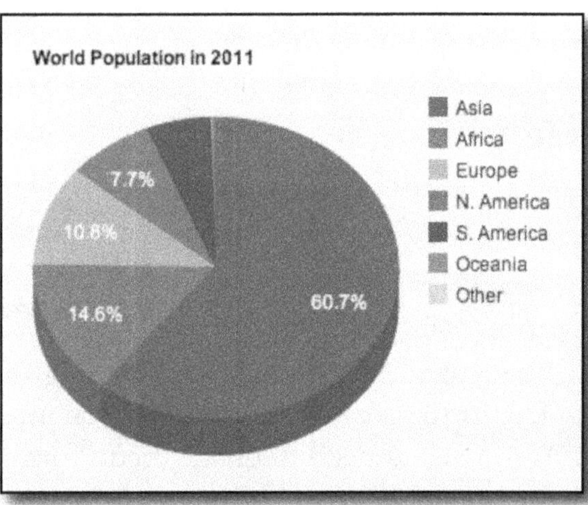

Class Project # 29
Excel: Graphs and Charts
WWW.PAULRALLION.COM

➢ Copy the tables from the handout and reproduce both Charts: "Motor Vehicle Production," and "2011 World Population." Make sure your charts are identical to the those on the handout.

Homework # 29
Excel: Graphs and Charts
WWW.PAULRALLION.COM

1.- What is the difference between Pie and Bar Charts?
2.- Why is the chart legend important?
3.- What are pie charts best used for?
4.- In a pie chart, what does the whole circle represent?

Sample Quiz # 29
Excel: Graphs and Charts
WWW.PAULRALLION.COM

1.- What identifies the data being charted through the use of color and shading?
2.- In a bar chart, is the Y axis vertical or horizontal?
3.- In a bar chart, is the X axis vertical or horizontal?
4.- In a pie chart, what does the whole circle represent?

Handout # 30
Microsoft PowerPoint®
WWW.PAULRALLION.COM

Objective: You will learn how to use Microsoft Power Point® to make an electronic presentation.

What would I need Microsoft PowerPoint® for?

➢ Knowing how to use Microsoft PowerPoint®, like all other programs, can be a life-long skill. You use PowerPoint® to make professional presentations using your computer.

Presentations Galore!

➢ When you open the program, you can either select a template, or you can start a blank presentation. Microsoft Powerpoint® organizes your presentations by slides, with animated text, enriched with pictures.

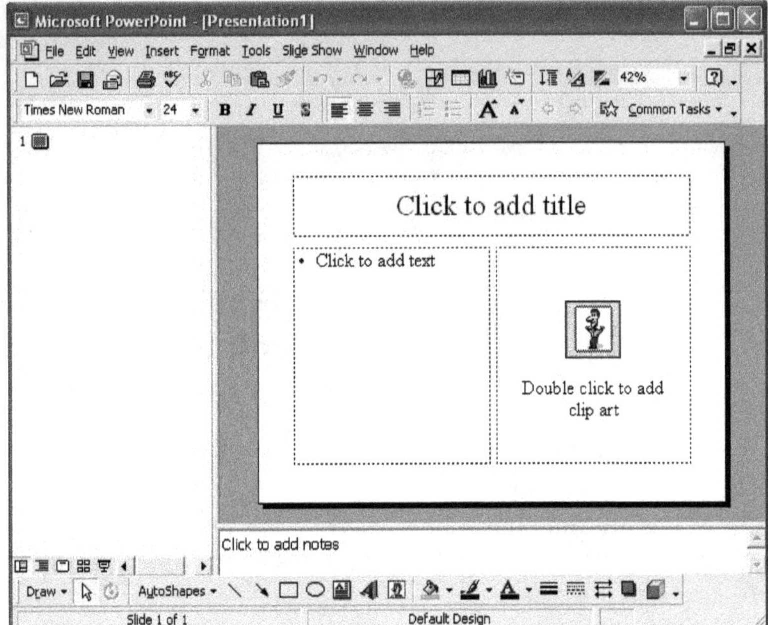

Inserting Graphics:

➢ New slides come with text boxes which you click in order to start typing. In addition, you can insert all kinds of graphics. From the Insert menu select a Textbox, WordArt, a Shape, a Chart, a Picture (from your computer or flashdrive), or Clipart (a set of cartoons and pictures that come with the program). You may also drag the picture file from your desktop or from another window, such as an Internet browser.

To set a picture as your slide background, cover the slide area and then cross-click on the picture, and select: Arrange ⇨ Send to Back. This will bring your text and other objects to the foreground.

Adding or Modifying Slides:

➢ You can now make changes to any slide, or add new ones. To make changes to a slide, select a slide number on the left pane and make changes on the right (on the actual slide). To add a new slide, go to Insert ⇨ New Slide, or Ctrl + M. You may change the order of the slides by dragging and dropping the slide icons on the preview pane on the left hand side. Make sure you save your work often!

To View Slide Show:

➢ When you are finished, click on Slide Show ⇨ View Show! You can also use a shortcut to start your presentation right away and impress your audience. To do this, press and hold the "Command" symbol (⌘), and press Return. ...enjoy the show!

Class Project # 30
Microsoft PowerPoint®
WWW.PAULRALLION.COM

➢ Make an electronic presentation about any topic of your choice. Make sure you have a Title slide, and at least four additional slides. Add some effects and transition to your slides.

Homework # 30
Microsoft PowerPoint®
WWW.PAULRALLION.COM

1.- What do you use MS PowerPoint for?
2.- How does MS PowerPoint arrange your presentations?
3.- How do you insert a picture into a slide?
4.- How do you make changes to a given slide?

Sample Quiz # 30
Microsoft PowerPoint®
WWW.PAULRALLION.COM

1.- PowerPoint organizes your presentation by:
2.- What is one way to insert a picture in PowerPoint?
3.- What is the command to set a picture as a slide background?
4.- Going from one slide to the next with some kind of effect is called:

HANDOUT # 31

PowerPoint Transitions & Animation

WWW.PAULRALLION.COM

Objective: You will learn how to add transitions and animation to your presentation.

Adding Transitions:

➤ Adding a fancy way to move from slide to slide makes your presentation more attractive. To add transitions, click on the "Transitions" tab below the Standard Toolbar (as shown below). Click on a slide, and then select the type of transition you'd like for that slide. To make changes to your transitions, click on the Options botton on the left. You can adjust the speed, sound (if desired), or whether you'd like a manual transition or automatic transitions every few seconds.

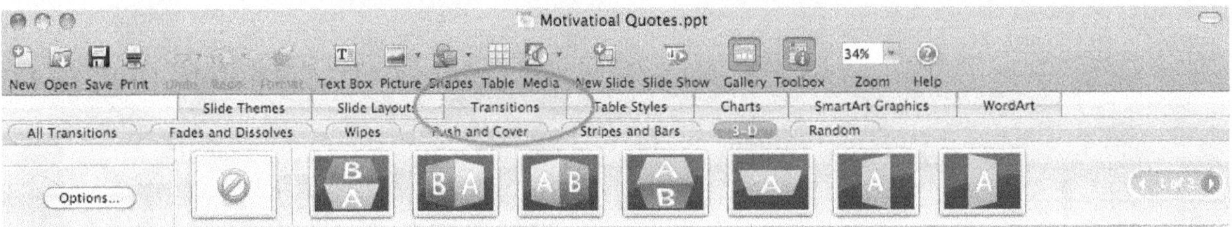

Adding Animation:

➤ You can add effects and animation by going to Slide Show ⇨ Custom Animation. You'll get your Formatting Palette (or Toolbox) opened in the 3rd tab with the Star icons. First, click the object you'd like to animate (a text box or a picture within a slide) and then select one of the following stars:

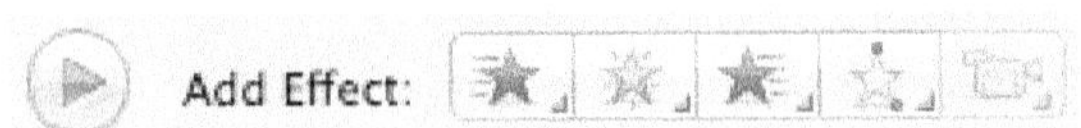

- The first Star adds Entrance effects (Appear, Fade, Fly in, Peek In, Rise Up, etc.).
- The second Star adds Emphasis effects (Shimmer, Wave, Change Font Color, Brush On Color, Blink, etc.).
- The third Star adds Exit effects (Disappear, Fade, Fly Out, Zoom, Descend, etc.).
- The fourth Star adds Path Animation (Line, Curve, Freeform, Scribble). This is a nice feature that allows you to design a path of motion of your object within the slide!

To preview the effect you selected within a slide, without having to enter into Presentation mode, click the blue triangle in the circle on the left hand side, or "Play."

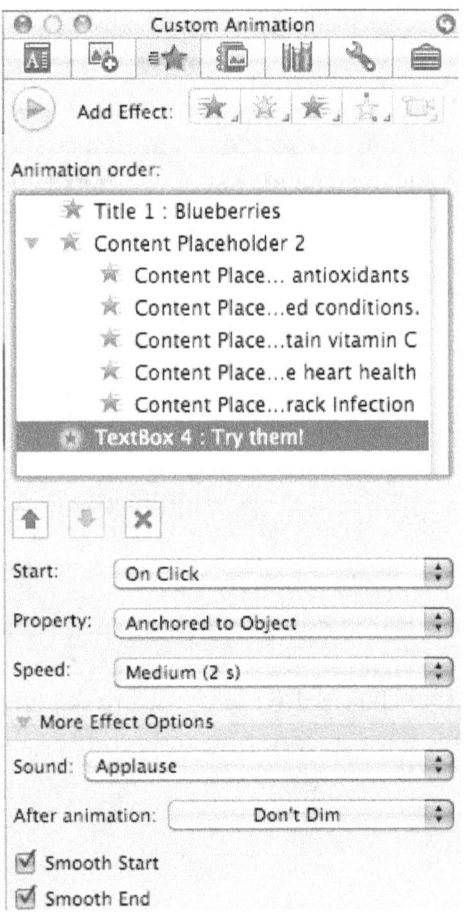

Inserting Other Cool Stuff:

➤ From the Insert menu, you can add a movie, sound, or music. You'll need the movie or music file, or you can record your own sound.

CLASS PROJECT # 31

PowerPoint Transitions & Animation

WWW.PAULRALLION.COM

- ➢ Prepare a fancy presentation with different transitions and animations.

HOMEWORK # 31

PowerPoint Transitions & Animation

WWW.PAULRALLION.COM

1.- How do you add transitions to your slides?
2.- How do you add animation to your slides?
3.- What are the four kinds of animation effects?
4.- How do you insert music or a movie?

SAMPLE QUIZ # 31

PowerPoint Transitions & Animation

WWW.PAULRALLION.COM

1.- A fancy way to move from slide to slide is called:
2.- What do you need to click on, in order to start an animation?
3.- Name on effect you can add to your slides:
4.- What other cool stuff can you add to your presentation?

Handout # 32
Sharing Your PowerPoint
WWW.PAULRALLION.COM

Objective: You will learn how to practice for and share your Power Point presentation.

Slide Show Timing:

➤ You can preset a certain amout of time for your slides (click the Transitions tab, click Options, set the amount of seconds per slide, and click on Apply, or Apply to All), or you can move along your presentation manually. To practice your presentation and give you an idea of how long you'll take for your presentation, you can Rehearse Timings. Go to Slide Show ⇨ Rehearse Timings.

Print Out Handouts:

➤ When you need your audience to have a handout of your slideshow, it is a good idea to print out the presentation a certain way. Click on File ⇨ Print, and you'll open the dialog box on the right. Next to: "Print What: Slides," you can select how many slides you can print out per page. The one that allows your audience to write notes next to each slide (the most useful option!) is: Handouts (3 slides per page). Look at the insert at right.

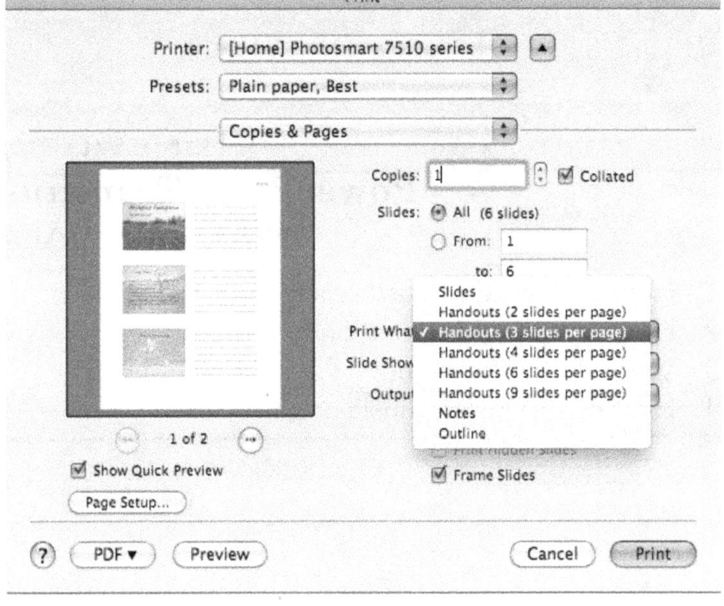

Share it in Other Ways:

➤ If you promise someone that you will "email" your presentation to them, you can send your original PowerPoint presentation.ppt file. However, if you have personal notes within slides (the bottom of each slide allows you to type notes), you have copyrighted material, or just stuff you don't want to share in original form, you can share pictures of your slides instead. Here is how you do it:

File ⇨ Save as Pictures. You will end up with a folder with one picture (.jpg format) for each slide.

File ⇨ Save as Movie. You will end up with a movie file (.mov) that will play each slide for a few seconds automatically. This movie file can be uploaded to YouTube, or social media.

File ⇨ Save as Web Page. You will end up with a Web page file (.html) that you can open with a web browser, just like a webpage.

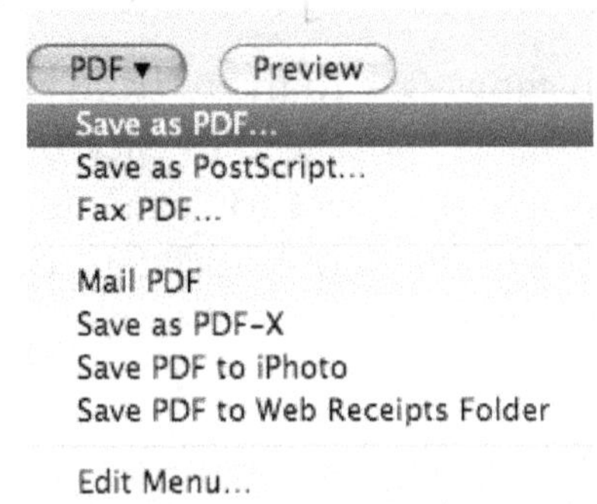

You can also save your presentation as a .PDF (Portable Document File). On the same Print menu above, click the PDF button and select: Save as PDF… (picture at right).

Class Project # 32
Sharing Your PowerPoint
WWW.PAULRALLION.COM

➢ Make a PowerPoint presentation and chose two different ways to share it with your instructor, and/or family and friends.

Homework # 32
Sharing Your PowerPoint
WWW.PAULRALLION.COM

1.- How do you practice for your presentation?
2.- How do you print out your presentation?
3.- What are other ways to share your presentation?
4.- How do you save your presentation as a PDF file?

Sample Quiz # 32
Sharing Your PowerPoint
WWW.PAULRALLION.COM

1.- Name one way you can share your presentation:
2.- Name another way you can share your presentation:
3.- How many slides per page allows for the audience to take notes on your handouts?
4.- Saving your presentation as web page lets you view it just like a webpage, True or False?

HANDOUT # 33
Electronic Mail, or e-mail
WWW.PAULRALLION.COM

Objective: You will learn the history and some tips to use electronic mail.

A Short History of E-mail

➢ People have always had the desire to communicate. E-mail is part of the Internet, the largest network of computers in the world. Telegraph messages and Morse Code transmissions are grand-parents of e-mail communication in that they are means of electronic messaging. During the 1970's and 1980's, personal computers became popular and in the 1990's, companies started to use email within their local networks for their employees to communicate. As the Internet became available to more people, email became a convenient way of communication.

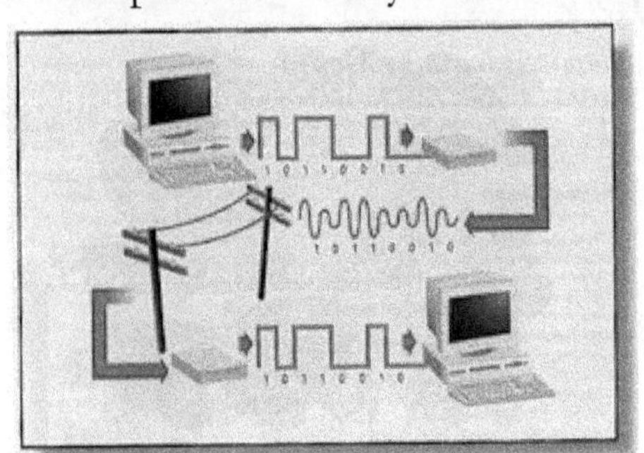

How do I use e-mail?

➢ You have two choices: One is to use web-based email, such as Google Mail, Yahoo Mail, MSN Hotmail, Mail.com, or you can use programs especially designed to handle e-mail: Microsoft Entourage, Microsoft Outlook, Apple's Mail, Windows Mail, etc.

What are the advantages of e-mail?

➢ E-mail is available world-wide; it is inexpensive and popular. The person receiving an email can read it and answer it at his/her own convenience.

What can you use e-mail for?

➢ People communicate about anything and everything across the globe via e-mail. You can also share pictures, videos, and send digital documents (such as Microsoft Word, Excel, or PowerPoint files) as attachments.

A few tips for e-mail use:

➢ Do not assume e-mail is completely secure.
➢ Do not send abusive messages. If you receive one, ignore it.
➢ Try to keep your e-mail messages short.
➢ Avoid upper case only. IT LOOKS AS IF YOU ARE SHOUTING.

➢ When attaching files, try to keep the file sizes down, maybe lower than 5MB, unless the receiver agrees to it. If sending a large picture or video, reduce it using the appropriate software.

What do I need so I can use e-mail?

➢ You need: a computer or smartphone with internet access, an ISP (Internet Service Provider) or Wi-Fi (Wireless Fidelity), and a web browser or e-mail program.

Class Project # 33

Electronic Mail, or e-mail

WWW.PAULRALLION.COM

➢ Do a research about the history of email on the web, things to avoid when using email, additional ways to protect yourself, etc.

Homework # 33

Electronic Mail, or e-mail

WWW.PAULRALLION.COM

1.- What became popular that helped to develop e-mail?
2.- What are the two ways to use email?
3.- What are two things you can use email for?
4.- What do you need in order to use email?

Sample Quiz # 33

Electronic Mail, or e-mail

WWW.PAULRALLION.COM

1.- What does the "e" stand for in e-mail?
2.- What year was email introduced?
3.- Name one advantage of using email.
4.- What is one thing you need in order to use email?

HANDOUT # 34
Email POP Setup
WWW.PAULRALLION.COM

Objective: To set up Apple's Mail® & Windows' Mail® to send and receive e-mail.

What is Apple Mail® & Windows Mail®?

➢ Apple Mail® (1st picture) & Windows Mail® (2nd picture) are email programs that not only send and receive electronic mail, but also allow you to manage your messages as well as your friends' email addresses. To POP (Post Office Protocol) your email means you download your messages and save them on your computer. One of the advantages of these programs is that you can work on messages and save them as "Drafts" without having to be online. Did I mention that these programs come free with Apple or Windows computers?

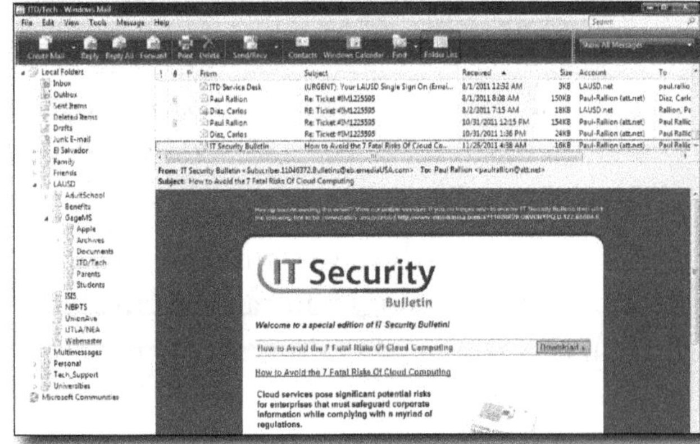

Set Up Your Email Account

➢ You can either use your email address with your Internet Service Provider (ISP), or your Gmail account. In general, follow the steps when you first open the program. Otherwise, select "Add Account" from the "File" menu. Either a dialogue to set up a new account appears, or a window like the pictures below. You need this information:

- Name, email address: username@gmail.com (if you wish to use a Gmail address).
- Incoming Mail Server: imap.gmail.com (or ask your ISP for this), and
- Outgoing Mail Server: smtp.gmail.com (or ask your ISP for this).

➢ Simple Mail Transfer Protocol (SMTP) is an Internet standard for electronic mail (e-mail) transmission across Internet Protocol (IP) networks.

➢ Using these programs doesn't mean you can't use the web-based email program.
You can use both!

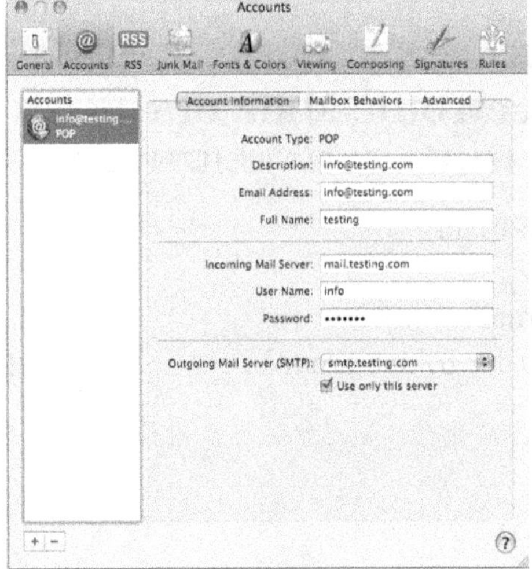

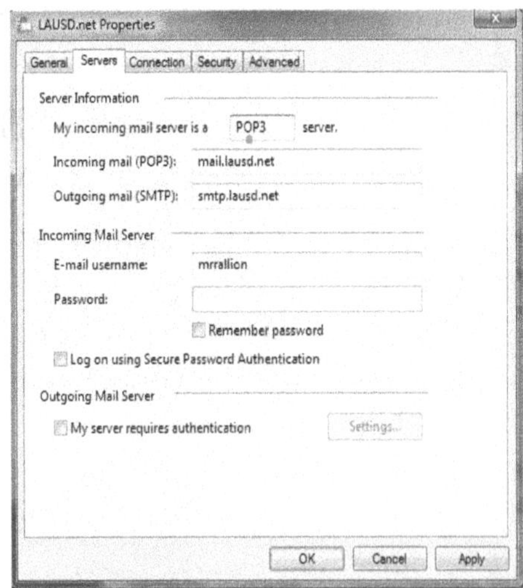

Class Project # 34
Email POP Setup
WWW.PAULRALLION.COM

➢ Depending on the kind of computer you have (Mac or Windows), set up your Mail program to send messages. Find out the proper settings from your internet service provider (ISP).

Homework # 34
Email POP Setup
WWW.PAULRALLION.COM

1.- What are the main functions of Apple & Windows Mail programs?
2.- What is one advantage of a dedicated e-mail program?
3.- How do you set up your email account?
4.- What does SMTP stand for?

Sample Quiz # 34
Email POP Setup
WWW.PAULRALLION.COM

1.- What does POP stand for in email set up?
2.- Where would you type an email address if you want to send a copy to someone else?
3.- Name one useful function of Apple Mail or Windows Mail.
4.- Using these programs can keep you from using web-based email. True or False?

Email POP

Objective: You will learn how to send and receive e-mail with Apple® & Windows Mail®.

Typing a Message (picture at right)

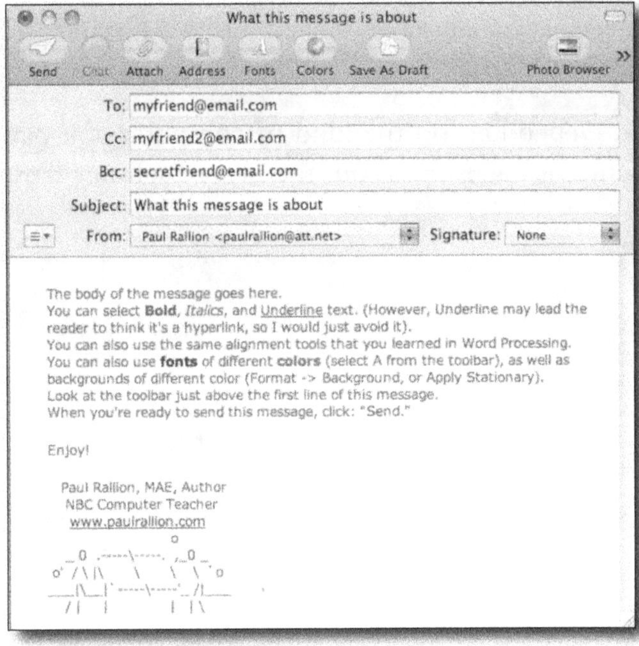

➢ Once you set up your email account, click "New Message" (Apple Mail, top right screen shot) or "Create Message" (Windows Mail, bottom right screen shot) from the toolbar. A new window pops up. Type the recipients email address in the **To:** field (and whoever you want to send copies to in the **Cc:** and **Bcc:** fields). From either program (Apple or Windows), you can use your Address Book* to import your friend's email address. Try not to leave the Subject field blank; put a key phrase or clue as to what the message will be about. As you type your message, you can format the words just like you do with a Word processor: **Bold**, *Italics*, Underline, text alignment, colored fonts, colored background, etc. Explore the toolbar for more options! When you're done, click "Send Now." To get your emails, click "Send & Receive." You can also check your message for spelling errors. In Apple Mail, Edit ⇨ Spelling and Grammar. In Windows Mail, click on ABC Spelling.

Attaching a File

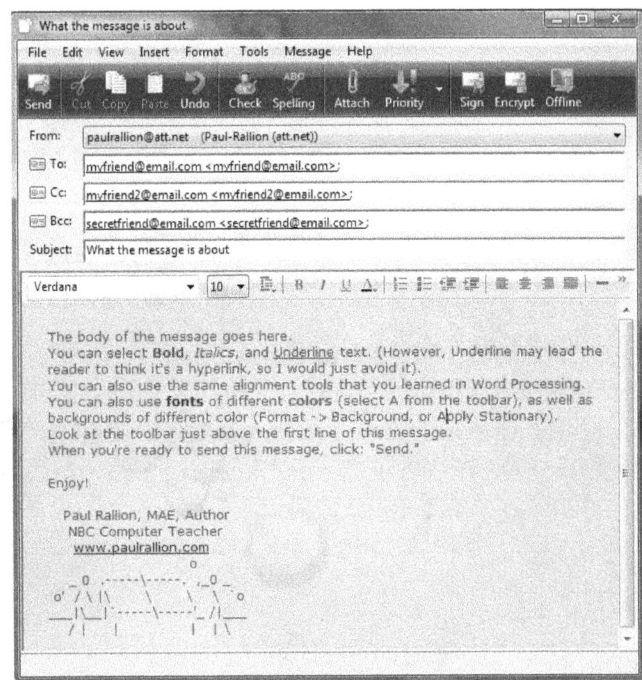

➢ To send a file attachment by email, such as pictures or documents, click on the paper clip (Attach). A pop up window appears to let you navigate to the file you wish to send. Click "Choose," and select the file you wish to attach. You may also drag files from the desktop, or from a Finder or Windows Explorer window.

**Address Book*

➢ As with the Web-based email Address Book, you can keep a list of your friends' email addresses. You can save their home address and phone numbers, work address and phone numbers, birthdate, even their picture, and other notes.

Class Project # 35
Email POP
WWW.PAULRALLION.COM

➢ Send an email message to a friend and add him/her to your contacts list. Try saving your email message in the Drafts folder and open it later. Try to format your message before sending it. Send a file attachment. Have fun!

Homework # 35
Email POP
WWW.PAULRALLION.COM

1.- How do you start typing a message in both programs?
2.- What is the Subject field for?
3.- How do you send a file attachment?
4.- What's the Address Book used for?

Sample Quiz # 35
Email POP
WWW.PAULRALLION.COM

1.- Where do you type a key phrase or clue as to what the message will be about?
2.- Where would you type an email address if you want to send a copy to someone else?
3.- Where do you click to send a file attachment?
4.- What's a list of friend's emails and other information?

HANDOUT # 36

Google Mail

WWW.PAULRALLION.COM

Objective: You will learn how to send and receive electronic mail using Google's web-based e-mail service: Gmail.

How do I log in to Gmail? (picture at right)

➢ First, go to: mail.google.com, click on: "Create an Account" and then enter your personal information. Come up with a unique username and password. You will need those to log in to your account. You email address is something like this: username@gmail.com

➢ Click on "Mail" so you can send, receive, and manage your emails. To get started and send an email, click "Compose Mail," and then fill in these fields:

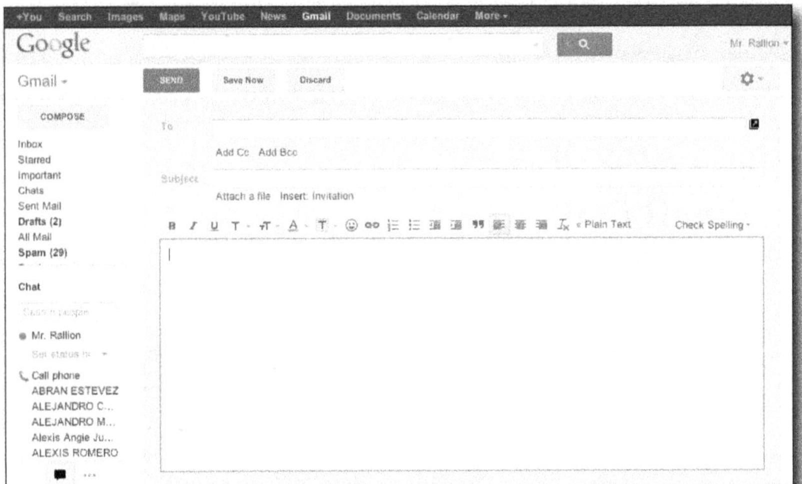

To: Type the email address of the person you wish to write to.
Cc: Use "carbon copy" if you wish to send a copy of this email to someone else.
Bcc: Use "blind carbon copy" if you wish to send a copy of this email to someone else, but you don't want the "To" and "Cc" people to know you're also sending "Bcc" a copy.
Subject: Give an idea to the reader what the email is going to be about.

The field below is for you to type your message. When you are finished, click: "Send." If you wish to send an attachment, click "Attach a File" and select the file(s) you wish to attach.

Contacts (picture at right)

➢ Click Gmail under Google and select Contacts. This is a handy agenda with email addresses and additional information. To add your friends to your contacts, click this icon: +. Instead of having to type your friends' email address every time you want to send them an email, just click To: and select their names.

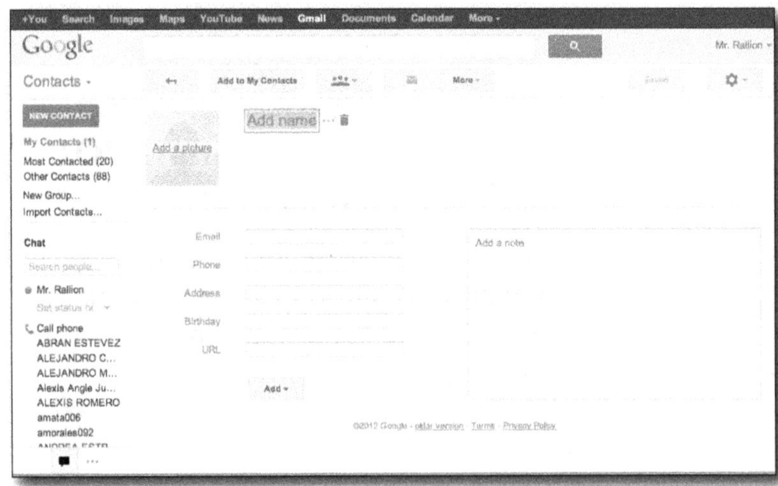

Class Project # 36
Google Mail
WWW.PAULRALLION.COM

➢ Send an email message to a friend and add him/her to your contacts list. Have fun!

Homework # 36
Google Mail
WWW.PAULRALLION.COM

1.- How do you log on to Gmail?
2.- What are To: Cc: and Bcc: for?
3.- How do you send an attachment by email?
4.- What is the advantage of using a list of Contacts?

Sample Quiz # 36
Google Mail
WWW.PAULRALLION.COM

1.- Where do you click in order to start a new e-mail message?
2.- E-mail recipients in this box are "secretly" receiving the same message as To: and Cc:
3.- A handy list of your friends' emails is called:
4.- Where do you click in order to send an attachment by email?

HANDOUT # 37

Introduction to Google Docs

WWW.PAULRALLION.COM

Objective: You will learn how to use Google Docs®.

What is Google Docs?

➢ Google Docs is a free, web-based set of programs that you can use online: word processing, spreadsheet, presentation, forms, and drawing. You can also collaborate with other users in real-time. You can get a free GMail account at: www.google.com

How do I log in to Google Docs? (picture at right)

➢ Go to: docs.google.com, and type your full email address and password. Your email address is something like this: username@gmail.com

➢ Once you sign in, click on "Documents" to create, upload, and/or manage your work. To get started, click on "Create New." You'll create one of the following:

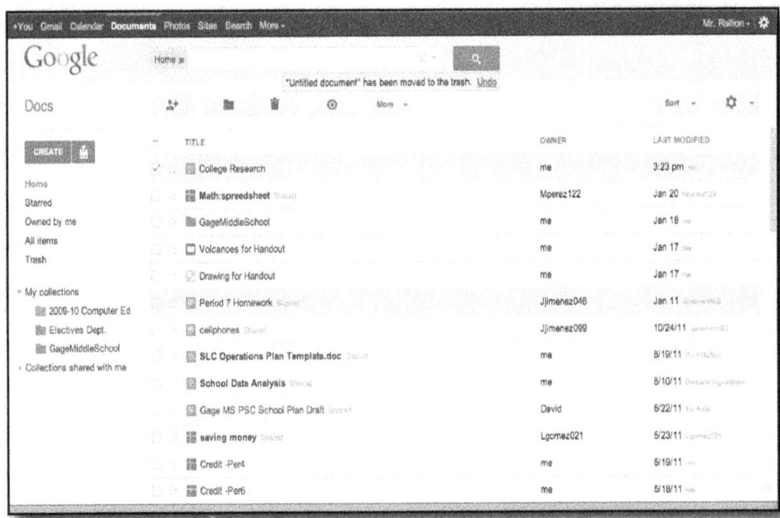

<u>*Document:*</u> This is a word processing document, like Microsoft Word®.
<u>*Spreadsheet:*</u> You can create a spreadsheet document, like Excel®.
<u>*Presentation:*</u> You can make electronic presentations, the same way you can with Microsoft PowerPoint®.
<u>*Drawing:*</u> You can make a Drawing like in Windows Paint® or Drawing®.
You can also click "Upload" to move one of your files (Word, Excel, PowerPoint, Drawing, etc.) to Google Docs and edit them.

Google Docs Advantages:

➢ Your documents are saved on the "Cloud," for universal access. You can access and work on the same document from different computers online, and you don't have to worry about backing your documents up.

➢ Google saves your documents automatically after every change you make.

➢ As the "owner," or file originator, you can click Share to grant access to other users so you can all work separately online, even if you are in different parts of the world. In the end, everybody contributes to the document. But can you tell who did more work? Yes! From the File menu you can select: "See Revision History" to see who typed what. Every member's contribution will be color-coded throughout the document.

➢ Finally, you can print, or download your Google Docs as Microsoft Word, Text, or PDF (Portable Document Format) files.

Class Project # 37
Introduction to Google Docs
WWW.PAULRALLION.COM

➢ Sign up for a free Google account and start a new Google Document. Create a new document and try working on it from different computers (from Mac to Windows and viceversa). See how you can work on the same document from different computes, ...even from different parts of the world!

Homework # 37
Introduction to Google Docs
WWW.PAULRALLION.COM

1.- How do I log on to Google Docs?
2.- Describe 3 kinds of Google Docs
3.- What is the biggest advantage of Google Docs?
4.- What are 2 ways that you can use Google Docs?

Sample Quiz # 37
Introduction to Google Docs
WWW.PAULRALLION.COM

1.- What is one kind of document you can create with Google Docs:
2.- The kind of Google Doc that creates a file like Microsoft PowerPoint is called:
3.- You can invite other Google users to work on the same document online, T or F?
4.- Name of the application to organize your schedule:

HANDOUT # 38
Google Docs: Word Processing
WWW.PAULRALLION.COM

Objective: You will learn how to use Google Docs® (Document).

How do I log in to Google Docs? (picture at right)

➢ Go to: docs.google.com, and type your full email address and password. Your email address is something like this: username@gmail.com

Google Docs! (Document)

➢ To get started, click CREATE to start a blank document, or click "Upload" to continue working on a word processing file, like Microsoft Word®. Remember, a word processor is used to write and format text: letters, memos, lists, keep a personal journal, your homework, reports, etc.

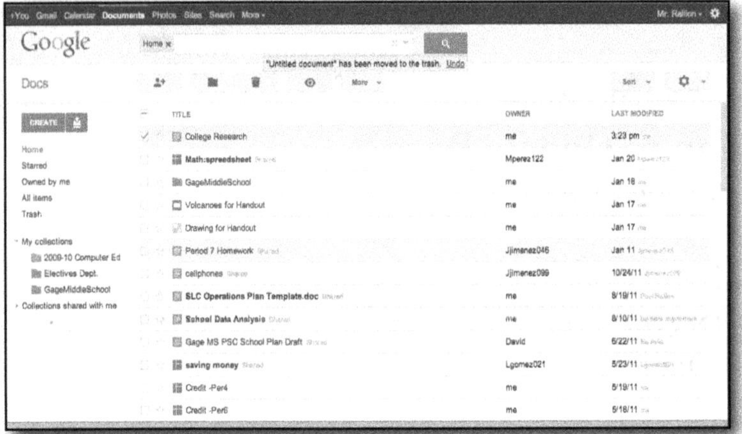

➢ You can change the font size, type, and color, as well as insert a link or an image. You can adjust the margins and tabs. In general, text in a word processing document looks the same on the screen as it does when printed.

Font formatting and alignment tools seem to be a simplified version of Microsoft Word.

➢ The toolbar looks like this:

Adding (text-wrapping) Pictures to your Document:

➢ Save a picture file on a folder you can later navigate to. Either go to Insert ⇨ Image and select the picture file, or click the double-mountain tool and select the picture file. To text-wrap it, click on "Fixed Position."

➢ You can finally print, or download your Google Docs to Microsoft Word, Text, or PDF (Portable Document Format) files.

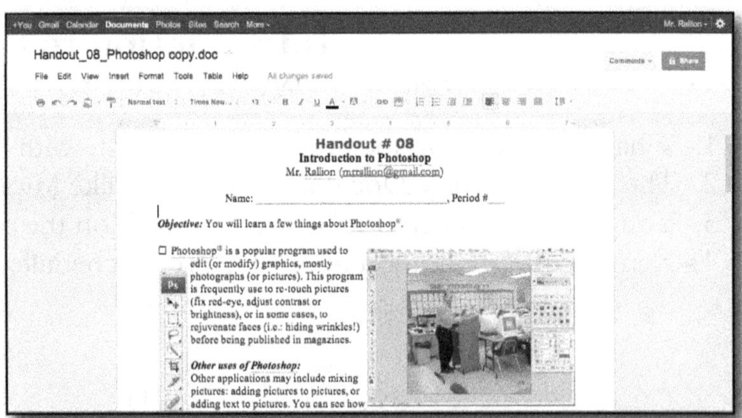

Class Project # 38
Google Docs: Word Processing
WWW.PAULRALLION.COM

➢ Start a new Google Document. Type a report (such as a project from school) and invite one friend to work on it together. Add a picture and wrap it with text.

Homework # 38
Google Docs: Word Processing
WWW.PAULRALLION.COM

1.- How do I log on to Google Docs?
2.- Describe the toolbar in Google Docs: Document.
3.- How do you add a (text-wrapped) picture to your Doc?
4.- What can you do when you finish your Document?

Sample Quiz # 38
Google Docs: Word Processing
WWW.PAULRALLION.COM

1.- Where do you click to start a new Google Doc?
2.- You can invite other Google users to work on the same document online, T or F?
3.- How do you insert a picture into a Google Doc document?
4.- How do you make a picture to wrap text?

HANDOUT # 39
Google Docs: Résumé
WWW.PAULRALLION.COM

Objective: You will learn how to type your résumé & sample letter of interest using Google Docs®.

Creating Your Resume:

➢ The word résumé comes from the French, *resumer*, meaning to sum up. Your résumé consists of four areas:

1.- Summary:
A good summary is a strong sentence highlighting your most notable accomplishments.

2.- Education:
List your education starting with the most recent accomplishment.

3.- Experience:
List your work experience starting with the most recent.

4.- Skills:
Do you have any interesting, but relevant skills? Add them here! Keep in mind that your résumé is one of many, and you want to impress your potential employer.

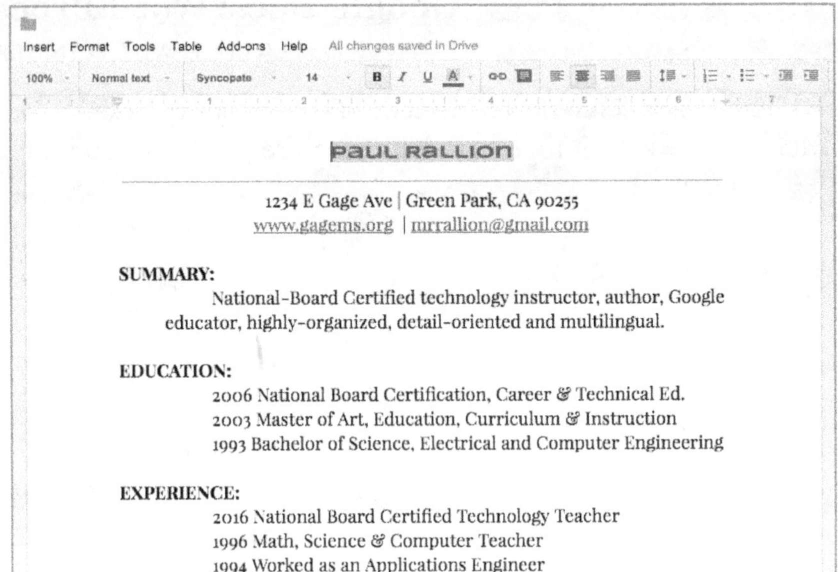

Letter of Interest:

➢ A letter of interest should address the needs of the job as described in the job listing. Pay attention to special requirements that you fulfill and add them there. Try searching online for sample letters as well. Here is a sample letter of interest you can use:

Dear Mr. Rallion,

I would like to apply for the position in technology that you have advertised.

I have a strong background in technology and the education and degrees to support it. I believe you may receive several applications, but my qualifications exceed your requirements.

I'm sure my skills would be a perfect match with your organization.

Sincerely,

Your Name

➢ If your letter and résumé catch the employer's attention, you may get a call for an interview. Do your research about the company and come prepared with questions.

Class Project # 39

Google Docs: Résumé

WWW.PAULRALLION.COM

➢ Pretend that you are looking for a job. Prepare your own résumé using a new Google Doc. Make sure to include the four areas as defined in class.

Homework # 39

Google Docs: Résumé

WWW.PAULRALLION.COM

1.- What does résumé mean?
2.- What are the parts of the résumé?
3.- What's a letter of interest?
4.- What should you do if you get a call for an interview?

Sample Quiz # 39

Google Docs: Résumé

WWW.PAULRALLION.COM

1.- The word résumé means:
2.- Name one area that your résumé must have:
3.- What is the name of the document you should send with your résumé?
4.- What is one thing you need to do for a job interview?

Handout # 40
Google Docs: E-mail Attachments
WWW.PAULRALLION.COM

Objective: You will learn how to send an attachment by email using Google Mail®.

There are three ways to send a Google Doc by email as an attachment:

1.- Download from Google Docs:

➤ Even though you can Share a Google Documents online, you can also download them. To do that, go to File > Download As and select one of the options: Microsoft Word (.docx), Rich Text Format (.rtf), PDF Document (.pdf), etc. Each choice has its own advantages. The advantage of downloading a PDF file is that the documnent will look exactly the same to the sender as it looks on your screen. By contrast, if you share a Word document with someone who doesn't have the same Fonts installed in his/her computer, your document may look different. However, if you wish to give the recipient flexibility in editing the document, Word becomes an easier file to edit.

2.- Drag files to send:

➤ You can drag a file from your Desktop, or a Finder or Explorer window. You need to have both windows open side by side (picture at right): the window for the email message, and the window where the file is. Drag the file onto the Gmail window, and you'll see a rectangular spot with the words: "Drop files here."

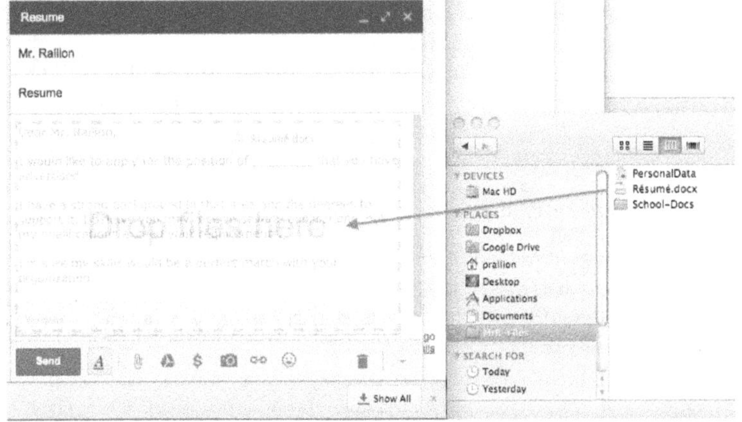

3.- Send an attachment by email:

➤ Another way to send an attachment by Gmail is to click on the paper clip: 📎. You'll need to "Browse," for your file, click it, and click on Open (picture at bottom right).

Other Attachments:

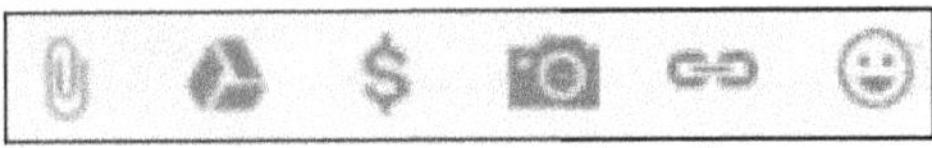

You can also attach files from your Google Drive (click next to the paper clip), insert a photo (click on the camera icon) from your computer or from the Web. You can also attach a clickable link (URL: Universal Resource Locator), which you can test right on the window. Finally, you can click on the happy face to insert an emoticon:

Class Project # 40

Google Docs: E-mail Attachments

WWW.PAULRALLION.COM

➢ Select one of your Google Docs, or start a new one. Send it to someone as an attachment using one of the methods presented here.

Homework # 40

Google Docs: E-mail Attachments

WWW.PAULRALLION.COM

1.- Which formats can you download your Google Docs in?
2.- What's one advantage of sending a PDF file?
3.- What's the easiest way to attach a file to Gmail?
4.- What other attachments can you send by email?

Sample Quiz # 40

Google Docs: E-mail Attachments

WWW.PAULRALLION.COM

1.- What kind of file attachment becomes easier to edit once received?
2.- What is the file format where the receiver looks at the document exactly as sent?
3.- What's the easiest way to attach a file to Gmail?
4.- You can send an emoticon by email. True or False?

Handout # 41

Google Docs: Spreadsheet

WWW.PAULRALLION.COM

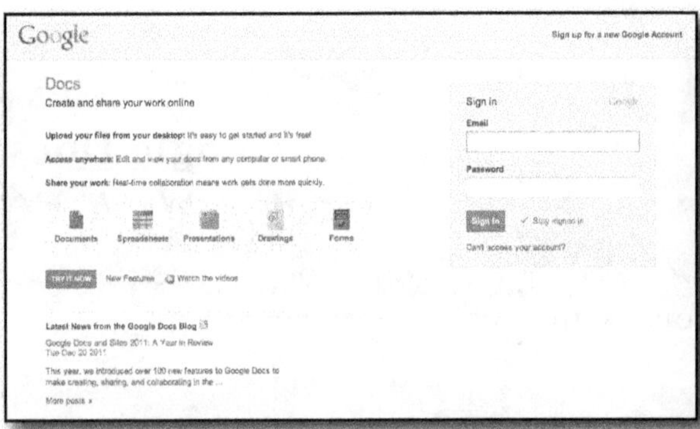

Objective: You will learn how to use Google Docs® (Spreadsheet).

How do I log in to Google Docs? (picture at right)

➢ Go to: docs.google.com, and type your full email address and password. Your email address is something like this: username@gmail.com

Google Docs! (Spreadsheet)

➢ To get started, click on CREATE to start a blank document, or click on "Upload" to continue working on a spreadsheet file, like Microsoft Excel®. Remember, a spreadsheet is an arrangement of rows and columns of cells used to enter, calculate, organize, and analyze information. Spreadsheets are used to prepare budgets, financial statements, inventory management, and calculate projections.

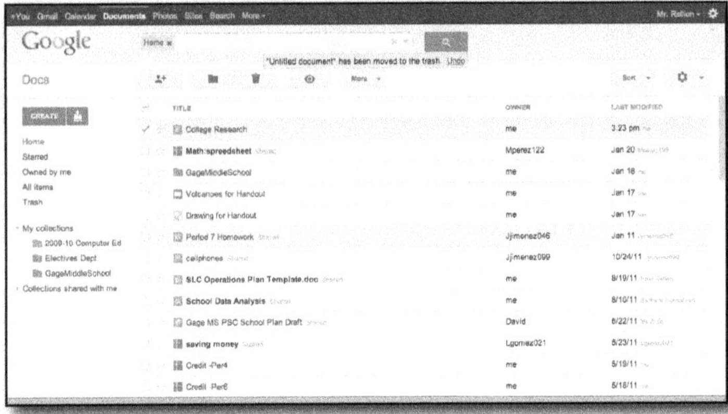

➢ You can change the font size, type, and color, as well as insert a link or an image. Font formatting and alignment tools seem to be a simplified version of Microsoft Excel. You can add a border or adjust the width of the columns (A, B, C, etc.) and the height of the rows (1, 2, 3, etc.). Click between them, and drag your mouse left or right, up or down.

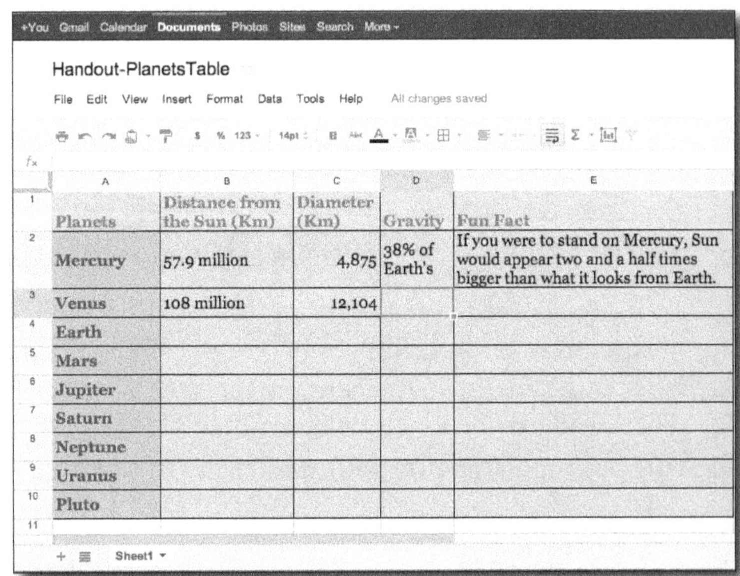

Planets	Distance from the Sun (Km)	Diameter (Km)	Gravity	Fun Fact
Mercury	57.9 million	4,875	38% of Earth's	If you were to stand on Mercury, Sun would appear two and a half times bigger than what it looks from Earth.
Venus	108 million	12,104		
Earth				
Mars				
Jupiter				
Saturn				
Neptune				
Uranus				
Pluto				

Applications:

➢ Google Docs adds an important ingredient to productivity: Collaboration. Let's say you need to set up a savings projection with a partner or even in groups. Instead of emailing a single document or pieces of text to be put together later (painfully), everybody contributes (from their own computer) to the same document that the owner Shares with other users. One or more users can input data and check everybody else's work. If necessary, collaborators can chat with each other to provide instant feedback. What do you think will be available in the future? How about Google Docs with video chat?

Class Project # 41

Google Docs: Spreadsheet

WWW.PAULRALLION.COM

➢ With a partner, copy the table from the handout and complete it with information you find online. Divide the work evenly. Have fun learning about the planets!

Homework # 41

Google Docs: Spreadsheet

WWW.PAULRALLION.COM

1.- How do I log on to Google Docs?
2.- What is a spreadsheet?
3.- What is another advantage of Google Docs?
4.- How do you adjust column width or row height?

Sample Quiz # 41

Google Docs: Spreadsheet

WWW.PAULRALLION.COM

1.- What is one kind of document you can create with Google Docs:
2.- The kind of Google Doc that creates a file like Microsoft Excel is called:
3.- What button do you click to invite other users to work on the same document online?
4.- Can you upload a Microsoft Excel file and convert it to a Google Doc? T or F?

HANDOUT # 42
Google Docs: Presentations
WWW.PAULRALLION.COM

Objective: You will learn how to use Google Docs® (Presentations).

How do I log in to Google Docs? (picture at right)

➢ Go to: docs.google.com, and type your full email address and password. Your email address is something like this: username@gmail.com

Google Docs! (Presentations)

➢ Click on "Documents" and then on CREATE to start a new file. From the drop-down menu select *Presentation* and you'll be starting an electronic presentation like in Microsoft PowerPoint®. You can also click "Upload" to copy one of your PowerPoint files to Google Docs.

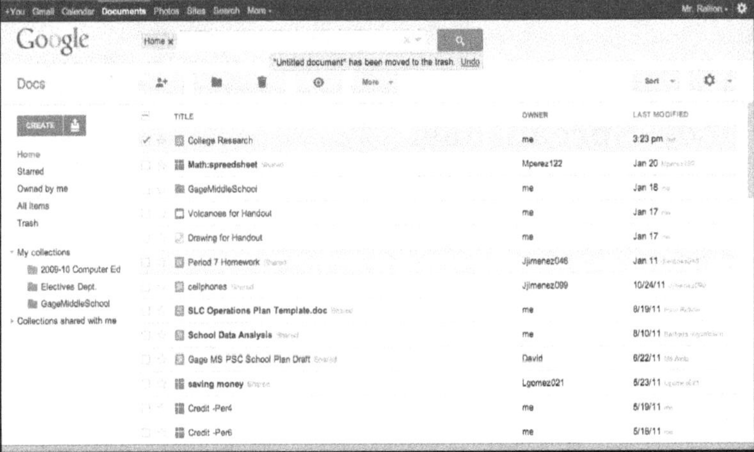

➢ When you start a new presentation you get a title slide. Follow the prompts: Click to add title, and subtitle. To add slides, click on the PLUS sign above the slide preview column on the left. As with other Google Docs, you can change the font size, type, and color, as well as insert a link or an image. Font formatting and alignment tools seem to be a simplified version of Microsoft PowerPoint.

Applications:

➢ Google Docs adds an important ingredient to productivity: Collaboration. Let's say you have to work on a presentation with a partner or in groups. Instead of emailing a file or pieces of text to be (painfully) put together later, everybody contributes to the same document at their own convenience, each from their own computer. The "owner" of the file Shares access with other users. Any user can finally print, or download the Google Docs Presentation as a Microsoft PowerPoint, or PDF (Portable Document Format) file.

Class Project # 42

Google Docs: Presentations

WWW.PAULRALLION.COM

➢ Make an electronic presentation using Google Docs. Invite one or more friends to collaborate. Make it as fancy as possible. After all, you are working as a group.

Homework # 42

Google Docs: Presentations

WWW.PAULRALLION.COM

1.- How do I log on to Google Docs?
2.- What is Google Docs: Presentations?
3.- How can you convert a PowerPoint Presentation to a Google Docs: Presentation?
4.- How do you add a slide to your presentation?

Sample Quiz # 42

Google Docs: Presentations

WWW.PAULRALLION.COM

1.- Where do you click to start a new Google Doc?
2.- You can invite other Google users to work on the same document online, T or F?
3.- How do you insert a picture into a Google Doc Presentation?
4.- How do you add a slide to your presentation?

HANDOUT # 43
Google Docs: Drawing
WWW.PAULRALLION.COM

Objective: You will learn how to use Google Docs® (Drawing).

How do I log in to Google Docs? (picture at right)

➢ Go to: docs.google.com, and type your full email address and password. Your email address is something like this: username@gmail.com

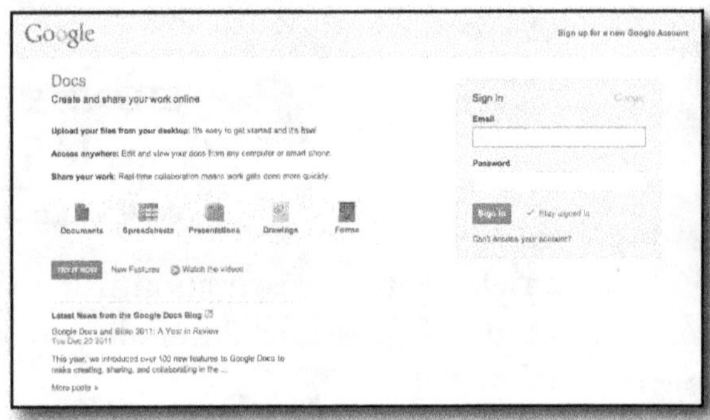

Google Docs! (Drawing)

➢ Click on "Documents" and then on CREATE to start a new file. From the drop-down menu select *Drawing* and you'll be starting a Drawing like in Windows Paint® or a Drawing program. You can also click "Upload" to copy one of your Drawings to Google Docs.

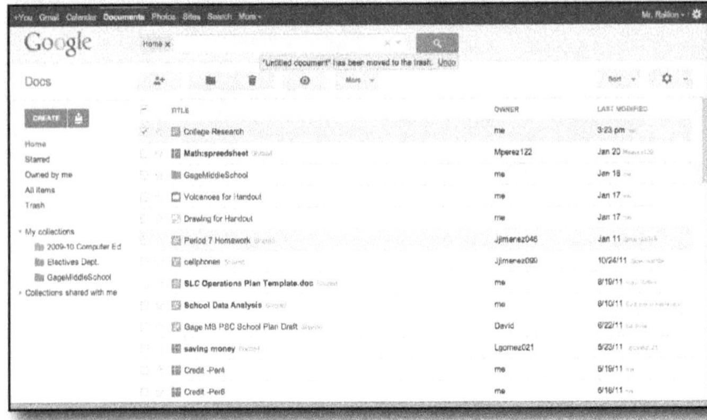

➢ When you start a new Drawing you get a checkered work area, which you can resize by clicking and dragging the bottom right corner. From the toolbar (next to the Select arrow) you can select one of the Drawing tools: Line, Arrow, Polyline, Arc, or Scribble. The next set of tools: Shapes, Arrows, Callouts (as in cartoon bubbles for dialogue!), or Equation. You may also click on "T" to insert text, or the double-mountain icon to add a picture.

➢ A drawing is made of "objects" –elements that can be moved or resized. When you select it (click on it), the handles appear. You can move the object when the "plus-sign-shaped" arrows appear, or resize the object when the single arrow appears. You can make copies of an object by using (Control-C) and (Control-V).

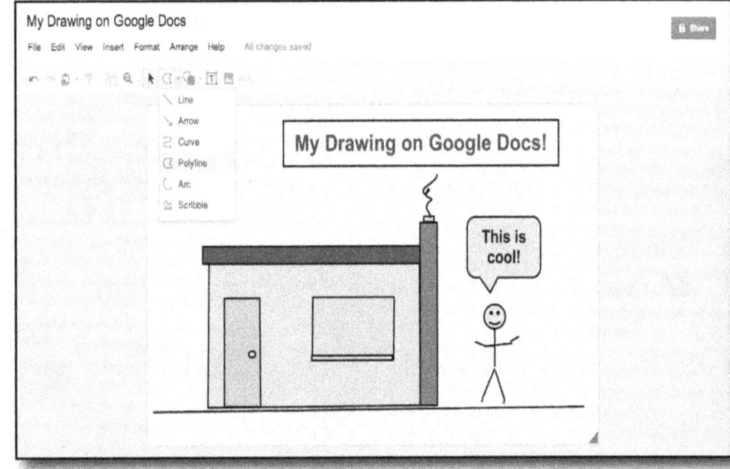

➢ Google Docs adds an important ingredient to productivity: Collaboration. Let's say you have to work on a drawing with a partner or in groups. Instead of drawing, scanning, and emailing a file or pieces of a drawing to be put together later, everybody contributes to the same document at their own convenience, each from their own computer. To do this, the "owner" of the file Shares access with the other users. Any user can finally print, or download the Google Docs Drawing as a JPEG (Joint Photographer's Group) file, a PNG (Portable Network Graphics) file, a SVG (Scalable Vector Graphics) file, or PDF (Portable Document Format) file.

Class Project # 43

Google Docs: Drawing

WWW.PAULRALLION.COM

- Make a drawing with a partner. Be as creative as possible!

Homework # 43

Google Docs: Drawing

WWW.PAULRALLION.COM

1.- How do I log on to Google Docs?
2.- What happens when you Create a new Drawing?
3.- What are "Objects"?
4.- What other formats can you save your Drawing as?

Sample Quiz # 43

Google Docs: Drawing

WWW.PAULRALLION.COM

1.- The kind of Google Doc that creates a file like Drawing is called:
2.- What button do you click to invite other users to work on the same document online?
3.- Elements that can be moved or resized are called:
4.- What formats can you save your Drawing as?

HANDOUT # 44
Google Sites
WWW.PAULRALLION.COM

Objective: You will learn how to make a web site using Google Sites® (web-based, web design).

How do I log in to Google Sites?

➢ Go to: sites.google.com, and type your full email address and password. Your email address is something like this: username@gmail.com

Google Sites! (Web Design)

➢ Click on CREATE to start a new site. Type a name for your site. Google Sites will give you a web address that looks something like this: https://sites.google.com/site/mycompuclass. You can either select a Blank page or use a Template. Click CREATE again to get started.

➢ To start building your new site, click on the pencil -Edit page(s)- (picture at right) to load the editor and start adding content to your site. The word processing tools appear:

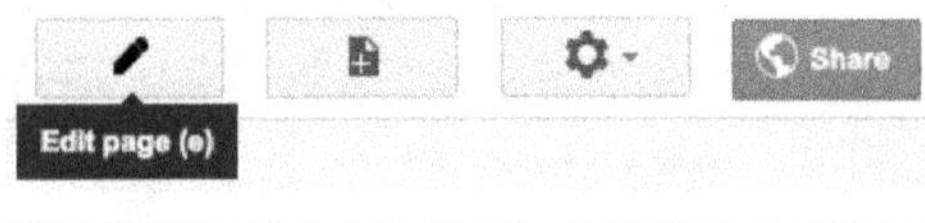

➢ Click an editable section of your page to make changes. Remember to click "Save." To add a page, click the button next to Edit: . Give your new page a name, and click CREATE. To modify your site, click on the toothed wheel: for More Actions (picture at right):

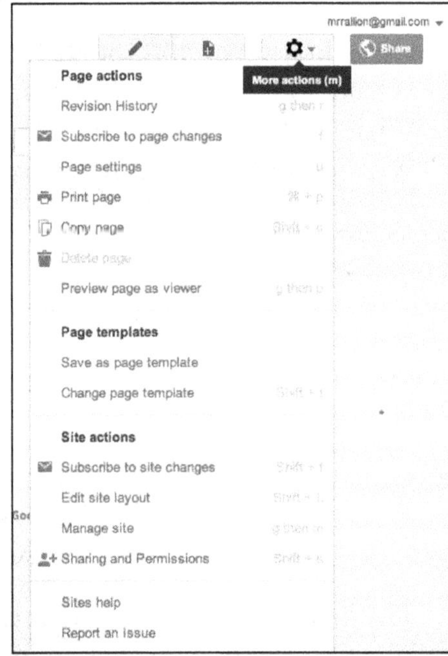

➢ Above the word processing tools, there are menus to help you improve the look and functionality of your site. For example, to add a picture to your webpage, click on Insert, and the drop-down menu below will be displayed. You will have the option to drag your picture file from the Finder, to browse your computer files, or from your Google Drive. You can also add a link to another site, a table of contents, etc. Please refer to the insert below:

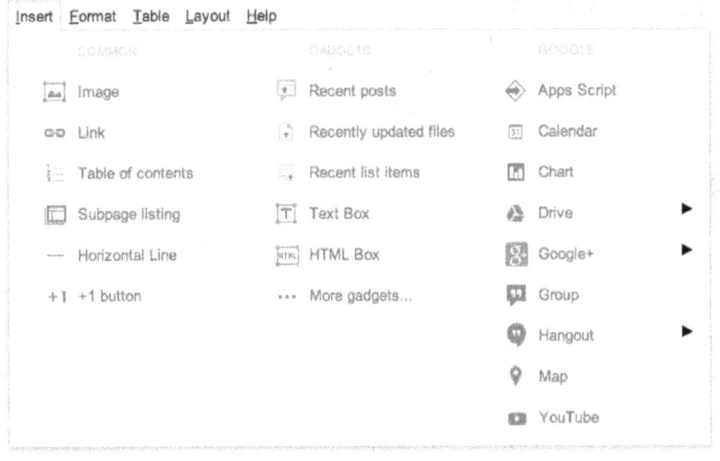

➢ As with other Google Docs, click Share to invite others to collaborate with you on your site!

➢ Tip: Open a new web browser window (command+N) or a new tab (command+T) to view your page, the way your visitors would see it.

Class Project # 44
Google Sites
WWW.PAULRALLION.COM

- Make a web site with a partner. Come up with the contents together, or divide the work.

Homework # 44
Google Sites
WWW.PAULRALLION.COM

1.- What would your Google Site address look like?
2.- What are the three tools that appear next to the Share button?
3.- How do you insert an image to your web page?
4.- How can you preview your web page?

Sample Quiz # 44
Google Sites
WWW.PAULRALLION.COM

1.- Which button do you click to start a new site?
2.- Which button do you click to invite others to work on the same document online?
3.- What is the command to add a picture to your site?
4.- How do you open a new browser window?

Handout # 45
Google Photos
WWW.PAULRALLION.COM

Objective: You will learn how to use Google® Photos and how to make a picture slide show.

What is Google® Photos?

➢ Google Photos is a service by Google® that allows users to upload, save and share pictures and videos. Once you upload them, you can make picture slide shows, photo collages, or movie presentations (which can be kept private, shared with certain people, or uploaded to YouTube). You can also view and share your pictures through your smartphone app, Google Photos.

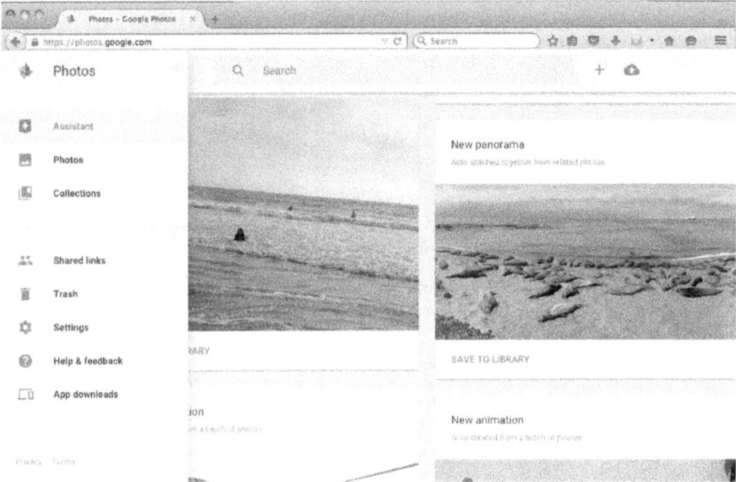

Uploading Pictures

➢ You can upload your photos and videos through photos.google.com. Log in to your Google Account by typing your full email address and password. You can drag and drop photos and videos to the center of the web page, or you can click on the upload button: . You have two choices: You can accept the image size Google sets (it's still high quality and you get free unlimited storage!), or you can upload your photos at full resolution that would count against your Google Account's 15 GB of free storage. Of course, you can purchase additional storage.

Google® Photos Online:

➢ You can view and manage your pictures and videos both on the Google Online platform and the smartphone app with these features:

1) Assistant: Google organizes your pictures and offers collages, picture stories, and animations, which you can save to your Photo Library.

2) Photos*:* All your pictures appear by date. You can also search your photos by: a) *People* (based on previous face recognition of your photos), b) *Places* (based on picture location), and c) *Things* (beaches, parks, etc.).

3) Collections: If your pictures and videos are saved in folders, the pictures appear grouped by Albums. Google Photos also groups pictures and videos by date or picture location (picture at right).

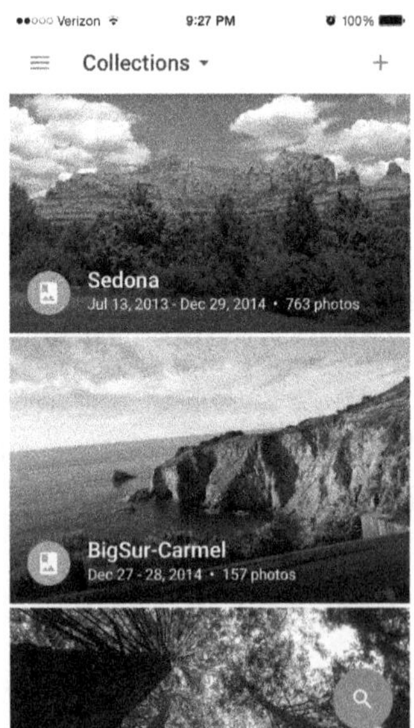

Smartphone App:

➢ From your smartphone, you can also access your photos using your Google Photos app, back up your camera pictures, edit, and share them.

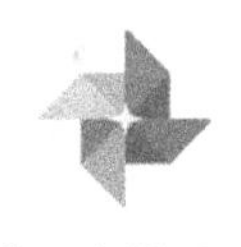

Class Project # 45

Google Photos

WWW.PAULRALLION.COM

- Try uploading your photos to Google Photos and explore Assistant, Photos, and Collections.

Homework # 45

Google Photos

WWW.PAULRALLION.COM

1.- What can you do with Google Photos?
2.- What are your choices when uploading pictures and videos to Google Photos?
3.- What features are shared in Google Photos and the Google Photos app?
4.- What can you do with the Google Photos app?

Sample Quiz # 45

Google Photos

WWW.PAULRALLION.COM

1.- With Google photos you can upload, save and:
2.- What is one thing you can do with your Google Photos app?
3.- What are the three major Google Photos features?
4.- What are three things you can do with Google Photos?

HANDOUT # 46
Picasa: Picture Tools
WWW.PAULRALLION.COM

Objective: You will learn how to use Picasa® to edit and enhance pictures.

Picasa Picture Tools:

➢ Picasa not only helps you upload your pictures to Google servers, it also allows you to edit them. Double click a picture and you'll get a window that looks like this:

The window is divided into three major sections:

1) Editing Tools: There is a plethora of options available! The first tab offers commonly needed fixes: Crop, Straighten, Red Eye, Retouch, Add Text, etc. The second tab allows lighting and color fixes. The third tab is for fun image processing: Sharpen, Sepia, Black & White, Film Grain, Tint, Glow, etc. The fourth and fifth tabs are more fun tools: Inverted Colors, Heat Map, Pencil Sketch, Neon, Border, etc.

2) Picture Preview: This is where you can see the modified picture and Apply changes if you like it. Click Cancel if you are not satisfied.

3) Picture Location Map: For location-enabled cameras, this section shows a map where the picture was taken. You can also view who is on the pictures!

Top Panel:

➢ At the top of the three panes, you can go back to your pictures, go back and forth in your picture series, or display two pictures in picture preview.

Bottom Panel:

➢ At the bottom of the three panes, thee are additional options to rotate the picture, send it by email, print it out, export it (save picture folder somewhere else), etc.

Class Project # 46
Picasa: Picture Tools
WWW.PAULRALLION.COM

- Select one of your pictures on Picasa and make two or more changes with Picasa tools.

Homework # 46
Picasa: Picture Tools
WWW.PAULRALLION.COM

1.- What are two things you can do with Picasa?
2.- What are the three major sections of Picasa?
3.- What can you do with the top panel?
4.- What can you do with the bottom panel?

Sample Quiz # 46
Picasa: Picture Tools
WWW.PAULRALLION.COM

1.- What is one thing Picasa allows you to do?
2.- What is one thing you can do with Picasa tools?
3.- Name one thing you can do with the bottom panel:
4.- For location-enabled cameras, what can you see on the third panel?

Handout # 47
Picasa: Picture Slideshows
WWW.PAULRALLION.COM

Objective: You will learn how to use Picasa® to upload pictures and make a picture slide show.

Picasa Slide Shows:

➢ In order to allow other people to view your pictures in the form of a slideshow, you first need to make your album visible (limited visibility or public). In order to do this, go to: picasaweb.google.com and log in to your Google account. Double-click an album, go to the drop-down menu: Actions, and select Album Properties. You can change the album information: Title, Date, Place Taken. Select Visibility: “Limited, anyone with the link” (Oval #1). Click on “Save changes,” and this will give you a “Link to this Album” on the right hand side of the screen (Oval #2). You can Copy/Paste this link to your slide show in an email, or a text message.

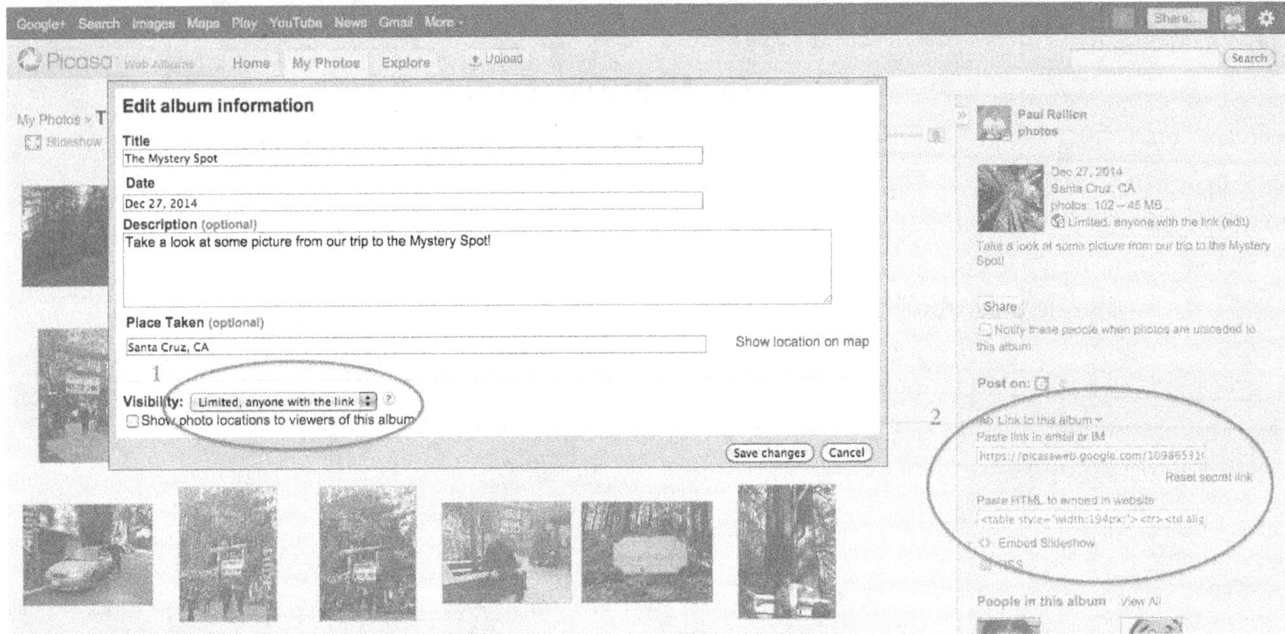

What does “Embed in website” mean?

➢ To “embed in website” means to display a live item on your website from another website. In this case, you can set up a slide show in Picasa and have it show in your website. In other words, you can embed your slideshow into your Google Site, for example. You’ll have to access the html code where you’d like to insert the slide show. To do this in your Google Site, click <HTML> on the tollbar and paste this code. Before you share your web address (sites.google.com/site/mycompuclass) with someone else, try it and make sure that it works.

Enjoy your slideshow!

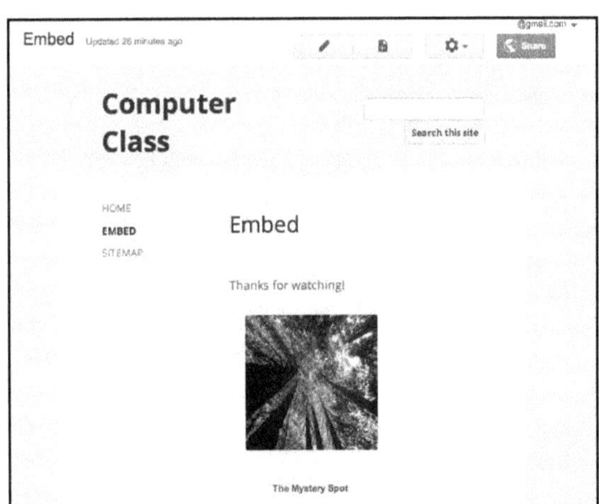

Class Project # 47
Picasa: Picture Slideshows
WWW.PAULRALLION.COM

➢ Try setting up a picture slideshow, share it with a friend or relative. In addition, embed your slideshow into your Google Site.

Homework # 47
Picasa: Picture Slideshows
WWW.PAULRALLION.COM

1.- What's the first step to allow others to view your Google Photos?
2.- How do you update your Album information?
3.- What does "Embed in website" mean?
4.- What are two ways you can share your Picture Slideshow?

Sample Quiz # 47
Picasa: Picture Slideshows
WWW.PAULRALLION.COM

1.- Before you can share your photos, you need to make your album:
2.- What is one way you can share your photo album?
3.- Displaying an item on your website from another website is called:
4.- What should you do before sharing your slideshow?

HANDOUT # 48
Google Calendar
WWW.PAULRALLION.COM

Objective: You will learn how to use Google Calendar®.

How do I log in to Google Docs? (picture at right)

➢ Go to: docs.google.com, and type your full email address and password. Your email address is something like this: uername@gmail.com

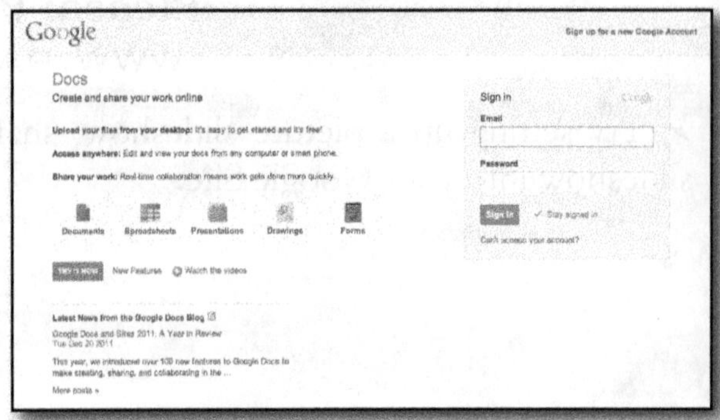

Google Calendar (picture at right)

➢ Once you log on, click on "Calendar." Google Calendars is a nice way to stay organized! For school: You can mark your homework due dates, school projects, and school events (like dances and games). For personal stuff: football practice, swimming lessons, dates, errands to run, etc.

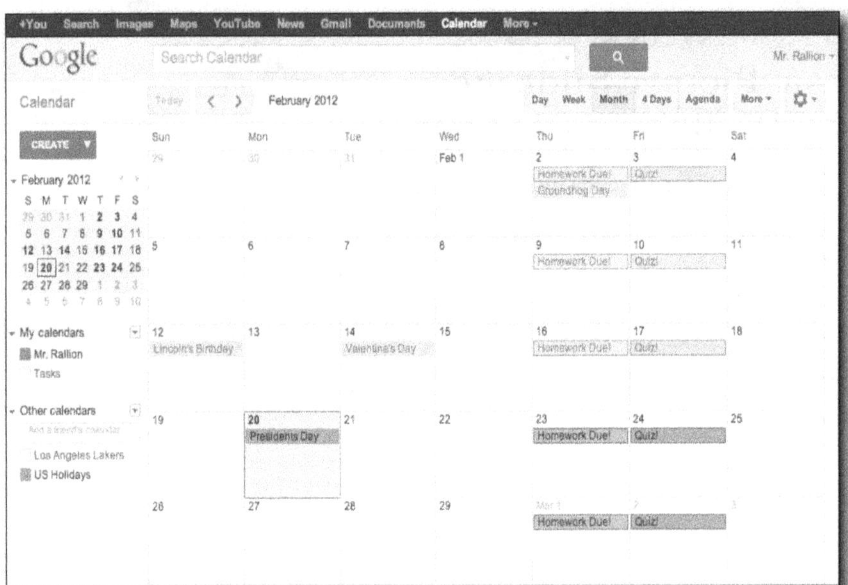

➢ You can also mark your friends' birthdates and have Google remind you so you can wish them *Happy Birthday*. Did you know you can load all the US Holidays, even your favorite's team season schedule? Just click on "Other Calendars" and "Browse Interesting Calendars."

Calendar Synchronizing

➢ You can synchronize your Google Calendar with your Smartphone (picture at right). You just need to download the application, or "app," sign in with your Google Docs account, and view or manage your events. The beauty of Google Calendars is that no matter what device you use to update your events, all other devices will be updated as well. Did I mention you can also access your Google Docs from your smartphone?

…what are you waiting for? *Try it!*

Class Project # 48
Google Calendar
WWW.PAULRALLION.COM

➢ Open your Google calendar and explore all its features. Look for interesting calendars and try Subscribing to them. Unsubscribe if you do not like one. If you have a smartphone, sync them!

Homework # 48
Google Calendar
WWW.PAULRALLION.COM

1.- How do you log on to Google Calendar?
2.- How is Google Calendar useful?
3.- How can you load US Holidays and sports schedules on your Calendar?
4.- How do you sync your Calendar to your smartphone?

Sample Quiz # 48
Google Calendar
WWW.PAULRALLION.COM

1.- What's the link you click on to start your calendar?
2.- What is one thing you can use Google Calendars for:
3.- How can you load all the US Holidays, sports schedule on your Calendar?
4.- What do you need in order to sync your Calendar on your smartphone?

HANDOUT # 49
Google Forms
WWW.PAULRALLION.COM

Objective: You will learn how to make a Google Form® to make surveys online.

How do I log in to Google Sites?
➢ Go to: sites.google.com, and type your full email address and password. Your email address is something like this: username@gmail.com

Google Forms:
➢ Go to your Google Drive and click on NEW to start a new Google Form. Google Forms are used to make free surveys. This can be a cool project with your family and friends. For example, you can ask members of your group in class what topic they want to do a project about. Or, you can ask your family members where they want to go on vacation and present a few choices.

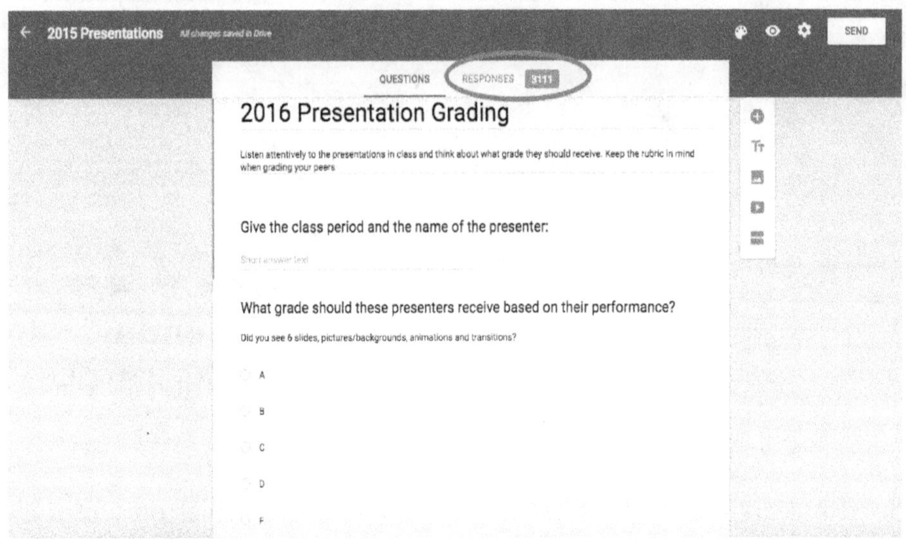

To Edit:
➢ Google has made it easier to edit certain sections by just clicking the word: "Untitled." Further, you can add a question, a title, a description, an image, a video, and another section by clicking the menu at right.

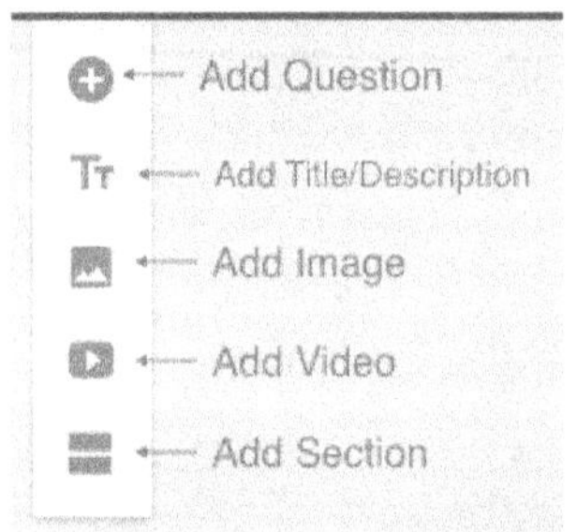

Ready? Send!
➢ When you're ready with your survey questions, click on the "Send" buttom at the top right. You can share your survey by email, by sending a Survey link, or by embeding an html code. You can also share your survey by Google+, Facebook, or Twitter.

➢ As people respond to your survey, you'll be able to see their responses. Look for the Responses tab enclosed with an oval on the top picture, next to the Questions tab. You can also see how many responses you have received. You can then view them with Google Sheets, print them out, stop accepting responses, get email notifications, or delete the responses, etc.

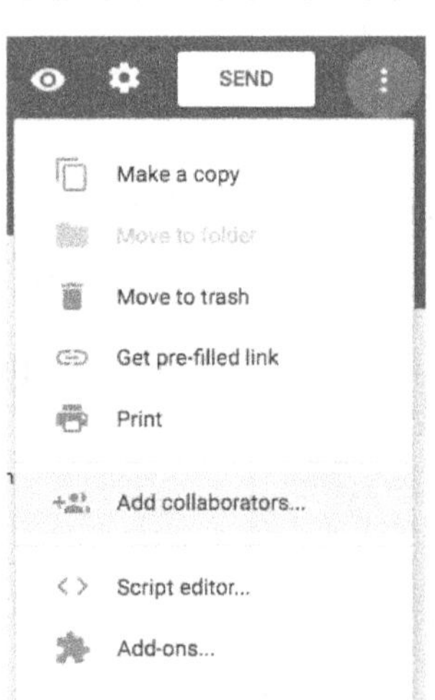

⋮ Click the 3 vertical dots (insert, bottom) to make a copy of the survey, move it to the trash, to invite others to collaborate with you, etc.

Class Project # 49

Google Forms

WWW.PAULRALLION.COM

➤ Open your Google account and come up with a survey using a Google Form! Tell your friends or family and have fun! Be creative, but also, be respectful.

Homework # 49

Google Forms

WWW.PAULRALLION.COM

1.- What are Google Forms?
2.- How do you edit Google Forms?
3.- How would you let others know your survey is ready?
4.- What other uses of surveys can you think of?

Sample Quiz # 49

Google Forms

WWW.PAULRALLION.COM

1.- What are Google Forms primarily used for?
2.- Name one way to let others know that your Google Form is ready:
3.- It is possible to collaborate online when usine a Google Forms. True or False?
4.- It is possible to stop accepting responses using Google Forms. True or False?

HANDOUT # 50
Files Across Devices
WWW.PAULRALLION.COM

Objective: You will learn how to save and access digital files across devices.

The Internet has made it possible to send files between computers, usually by email or through FTP (file transfer protocol). There is another way to send, or rather, SHARE files across devices through the Internet. It's called cloud computing.

➢ **Cloud Computing:**

You can start working on a document with one device (computer, tablet, or smartphone), and you can then access and continue to work on the same document where you left off with another device. You can also store, access, and share pictures, videos, audio files, etc.

There are many services online that are available. Some companies offer a few Gigabytes for free, but you can also purchase larger amounts of storage, depending on your needs. Some examples are: Box.com, Dropbox.com, Apple's iCloud, Google Drive, Microsoft's OneDrive.com, etc.

Keep in mind that to fully use those services, you'll need to install a "drive" on your computer, sort of like a "flashdrive," except the files are saved both on your computer and online. The beauty of this is that you can access and modify your files online. The drive becomes part of your Apple's Finder or Windows' Explorer. The back up is done automatically, although you can set different variables under that drive's preferences.

➢ **File Backups:**

There are other services that allow you to back up and access your files across devices. However, their focus is backing up your files, rather than online collaboration. These services include Carbonite, Mozy, and Backblaze.

These services will automatically (or allow you to manually) back up your files and allow you to recover files (by downloading them), in case of a disaster. However, it's not designed to give you editing privileges from your other devices. There are different levels of services, personal and business plans, what they cover, file size limit, telephone versus online support, etc. Before picking a service, do your research and go with the best service suited to your needs.

Class Project # 50
Files Across Devices
WWW.PAULRALLION.COM

➢ Sign up for free storage online with one of the companies presented here. Try transferring files form one device to another with the same account, or share documents with friends and family.

Homework # 50
Files Across Devices
WWW.PAULRALLION.COM

1.- What is cloud computing?
2.- What are some examples of backup services?
3.- What is required in order for you to fully utilize the cloud computing services?
4.- What's the difference between cloud computing and pure backup?

Sample Quiz # 50
Files Across Devices
WWW.PAULRALLION.COM

1.- Sharing and working on files across devices is called:
2.- Name one cloud computing company:
3.- What do you need to install so that you can fully use cloud computing?
4.- What can you not do with purely backup services when using other devices?

The Internet

WWW.PAULRALLION.COM

Objective: You will learn what the Internet is.

A Short History of The Internet

➢ The Internet is the largest network of computers in the world. In the 1960's the U.S. Department of Defense developed a networking project to maintain communications via computers in the U.S. in case of a nuclear attack. The original name for the Internet was ARPANET (Advanced Research Projects Agency NETwork). In 1972 the electronic mail (e-mail) was introduced. The World Wide Web came into being in 1992. In 1993 the world's first browser, Mosaic, was released.

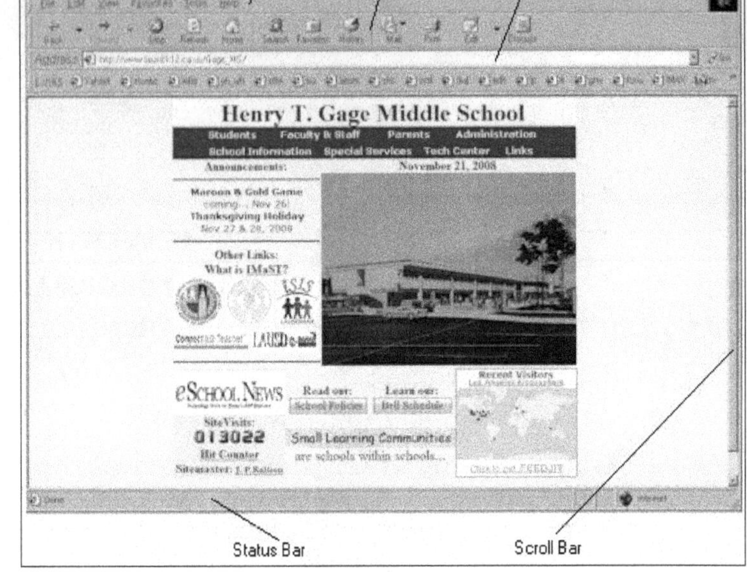

What is a Browser?

➢ A browser is a program used to retrieve documents from the world wide web (www or Web) and to display them in a readable format. Today, the most popular browsers are: Chrome (by Google), Safari (by Apple), Internet Explorer (by Microsfot), and Firefox (by Mozilla). The figure on the right shows you the parts of a browser.

Is the Internet and the www the same?

➢ No, the World Wide Web is part of the Internet. Also, parts of the Internet are: e-mail, newsgroups, the cloud (servers connected to the internet that allow you to save and access data), and ftp (file transfer protocol) –a way to send files or data over the Internet.

Web page extensions

➢ There are several web page extension, depending on what kind they are:
.com (commercial), .net (network organization), .org (organization), .edu (educational), .gov (government), .mil (military).
International URL's sometimes include a two-letter code for the country of origin. For example, www.estadao.com.br (Brazil), www.elmundo.sv (El Salvador), www.lemonde.fr (France).

How do I access the Internet?

➢ You need the following: a smart phone, a table, or a computer with a modem, DSL (digital subscriber line), or Wi-Fi (wireless fidelity), an ISP (Internet Service Provider), telecommunications software, and a web browser.

CLASS PROJECT # 51
The Internet
WWW.PAULRALLION.COM

➢ Go online and read about the history of the Internet. What new web page extensions have been developed?

HOMEWORK # 51
The Internet
WWW.PAULRALLION.COM

1.- What are the parts of the internet?
2.- List the webpage extensions from your handout:
3.- What things do you need to access the internet?
4.- What do you think the internet will be like in 20 years?

SAMPLE QUIZ # 51
The Internet
WWW.PAULRALLION.COM

1.- What was introduced first, email or the World Wide Web?
2.- The internet is made up of many parts. What is one of them?
3.- Name one thing you need to access the internet:
4.- What does the web page extension ".com" mean?

Handout # 52
Bookmarks
WWW.PAULRALLION.COM

Objective: You will learn how to manage bookmarks and synchronize (sync) them across devices.

➢ What is a Bookmark?

A bookmark symbolizes the familiar 4-inch laminated cardstock strip that you place between pages in a book to remember the last page you read. You don't want to flip through several pages to find out where you left off. Likewise, if there is a webpage that you like and inted to visit again later, you can "bookmark" it. Go to Bookmark and select "Bookmark this Page" or a similar command, depending on your web browser. You'll have two choices as to where to place the bookmark:

1. Bookmark Toolbar:

You can have a toolbar with your favorite bookmarks, those that you visit every day, for example. This bar is just below the address bar, and you can access your websites with one click:

2. Bookmark Folders:

If you find a web page that you think you may want to visit in the future, you may bookmark it in a folder. You can create as many folders as you'd like, just like in Apple's "Finder" or Window's "Explorer." You can create a folder first and then add bookmarks to it, or you can create a folder at the time you add a bookmark.

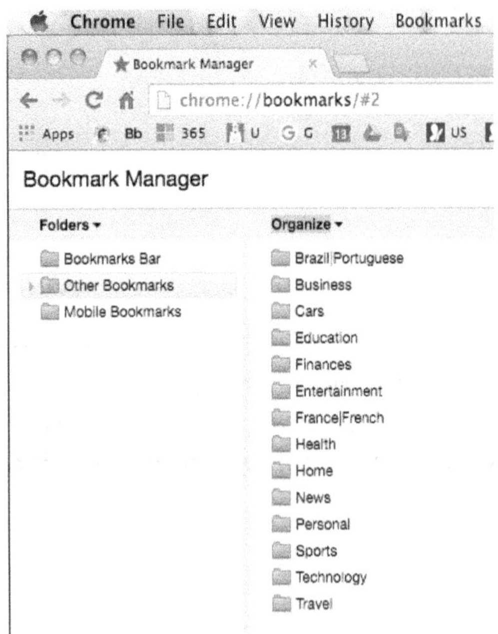

➢ One of the nice features of Bookmarks is that you can synchronize them across devices. Just make sure that you are using the same web browser on all devices, i.e.: Google Chrome, Apple's Safari, etc. Also, you'll need to sign in to the same account on that browser: Your Google Account for Chrome and your iCloud account for Safari.

➢ To Edit Your Bookmarks:

To edit your bookmarks, go to the bookmarks menu and select Bookmark Manager. You'll get the window on the right and you can then drag, drop, or delete bookmarks as you please. You can also go to the bookmark by navigating to it in the browser, cross-click and select Edit. You can then rename or delete your bookmark.

Class Project # 52
Bookmarks
WWW.PAULRALLION.COM

➢ Browse some webpages you enjoy and bookmark them. Once you have a few bookmarks created, organize them by group, in folders.

Homework # 52
Bookmarks
WWW.PAULRALLION.COM

1.- What is a bookmark?
2.- What's the difference between bookmark toolbar and bookmark folder?
3.- How do you organize your bookmark folders?
4.- How do you edit your bookmarks?

Sample Quiz # 52
Bookmarks
WWW.PAULRALLION.COM

1.- A way to mark a webpage in order to visit it later is:
2.- Bookmark pages you visit often would be best placed on the:
3.- Bookmark pages you do not visit as often would be best placed on the:
4.- You can sync your bookmarks across devices: True or False?

Handout # 53
Online Safety
WWW.PAULRALLION.COM

Objective: You will learn how to protect yourself online as well as manage passwords.

➢ **Personal Profiles:**

When you come across a website that asks you for personal information, you want to make sure it's a legitimate and secure website. You can tell by the web address; it should be https:// instead of http:// - the "s" stands for secure. Do you remember what http stands for?

In addition, you should see the Company name and a lock next to the web address. This means that the site uses certificates of authenticity to let you know it's legitimate: TLS (Transport Layer Security) or SSL (Secure Sockets Layer). Also, make sure the web address is official and does not contain an extra letter or character. For example, if you're looking at a bank's website, make sure it's their official website (bank.com), and not something like bank1.com.

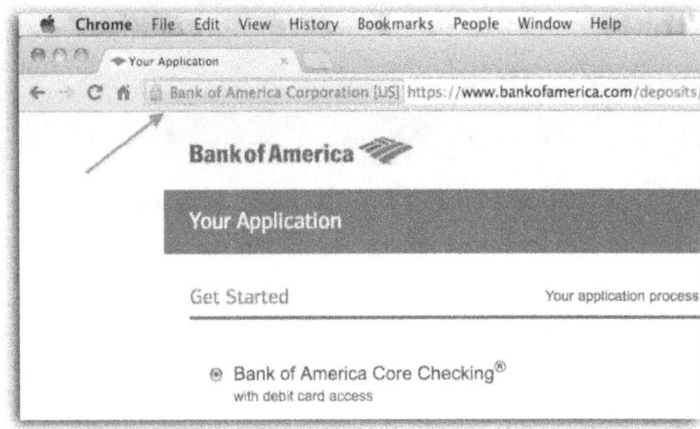

➢ **Hackers:**

Hackers may send emails to people telling them that their pasword has expired and needs to be reset. They provide a link that looks legitimate, and when you click on it (by the way, DO NOT CLICK ON IT!), it takes you to a website that looks official, but it's not. If you get an email like that, it's best to call your bank, or institution you may do business with, to verify if it's legitimate.

➢ **Sharing Info:**

Be careful with what information you share with people. Keep in mind that once you post something on the Internet and people download it, you can't get it back! For example, once you send a picture to someone by text or email, you no longer have control of it! You have no control of what they do with that picture. Try not to share your last name, your address, telephone number, date of birth, or other identification numbers. Why not?

➢ **Identity Theft:**

When someone gets a hold of enough information belonging to another person, they can assume their identity and apply for credit in their name without the victim's knowledge.

➢ **Passwords:**

When you sign up for an account online, it usually asks you for a password. Use a strong password that includes upper and lower case letters and numbers. But, how do you keep track of the passwords? There is no simple answer, and it depends on what works for you. One idea that may help you is to begin or end each password with the first letter of the business that you have an account with.

Class Project # 53
Online Safety
WWW.PAULRALLION.COM

➢ Discuss with friends and family the importance of online safety. Tell them about the importance of keeping their personal information private, and not replying to emails asking for it.

Homework # 53
Online Safety
WWW.PAULRALLION.COM

1.- How can you tell if a website is secure or not?
2.- Define the word Hacker.
3.- Why is it important not to share your personal information?
4.- Give advice to a friend on how to come up with a strong password.

Sample Quiz # 53
Online Safety
WWW.PAULRALLION.COM

1.- How can you tell if a website is secure or not?
2.- When you post a picture online, do you have control over who gets it?
3.- When somebody uses someone else's personal information to gain credit, it's called:
4.- What's identity theft?

Handout # 54

Social Media and Netiquette

WWW.PAULRALLION.COM

Objective: You will learn about Social Media and Netiquette.

Social Media:

Interactive web sites where thousands (even millions) of people have joined to find friends and share information, including pictures, music, videos, etc. These interactions happen online, hence the name Social Media. When used properly, it can be a fun way of staying in touch with family and friends.

➢ Facebook: As of the writing of this handout, Facebook is the most popular social media web site. You sign up for an account at: www.facebook.com, look for people you know, and send them requests to be your friends. When they accept your request, you can see their posts and they can see yours.

➢ Twitter: It works about the same way as Facebook, except each post is limited to 140 characters. To sign up, go to: www.twitter.com.

When posting a message, be aware that the information you share can be viewed by more people than you might want to, even if you have set your privacy settings to "High." Don't say anything that might come back and haunt you down the road.

➢ What is a blog?

A blog is a service that allows people to post content to a Web site, sort of like a journal. The contents of the blog are usually organized by posting, with the most recent on top. Google offers a free blog service at: www.blogger.com.

Netiquette:

Chewing with your mouth open is not good dining etiquette. Sending a virus to a friend with the intention to harm his/her computer would be an obvious no-no. Good behavior online is called Netiquette. Here are a few more pointers on how to behave online:

⇨ Just because your parents might not be watching, it doesn't mean others aren't. Follow this rule of thumb: Do not type anything you wouldn't type if your parents were watching you.

⇨ Email is not a fully secure way of communication. Do not send sensitive information that could put your identity in danger of being stolen. Do not reply to emails that ask for your personal information, account names and passwords. Many credit card and bank accounts have been compromised this way.

⇨ Email should have a Subject header that reflects the content of the message.

⇨ Do not use UPPERCASE LETTERS, it seems as if you are angry, or yelling.

⇨ When sending file attachments, do not send large files. Keep them under 5 Megabytes (MB), unless the receiver agreed to it.

➢ Computer Use:

Having access to a computer does not give you the right to violate other people's rights. Follow the Golden Rule: do not do anything that you wouldn't want to be done to you.

Class Project # 54

Social Media and Netiquette

WWW.PAULRALLION.COM

➢ Discuss the influence of Social Media in our society. Talk about the advantages of using Social Media as well as the consequences of abusing it. What are some important etiquette items?

Homework # 54

Social Media and Netiquette

WWW.PAULRALLION.COM

1.- What is Social Media?
2.- What is the difference between E-mail and Social Media?
3.- What is Netiquette? Give one example.
4.- What is a blog?

Sample Quiz # 54

Social Media and Netiquette

WWW.PAULRALLION.COM

1.- Name of the most popular Social Media site where you befriend others:
2.- Name of the Social Media site where each post is limited to 140 characters:
3.- What do UPPER CASE LETTER make your text look like?
4.- Name of the service that lets people post content to a Web site, like a journal:

Web Page Design

WWW.PAULRALLION.COM

Objective: You will learn how to create a link to make your own web page.

What is a Web Page Editor?

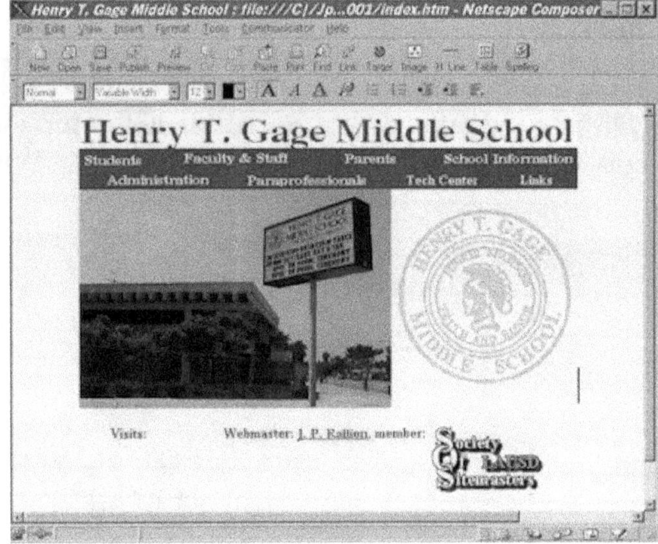

➢ An Internet browser is used to "read" webpages. Well, what programs are used to "write" those web pages? The answer is: Web page Editors, which use a universal language called *HTML* (Hyper Text Markup Language). You can develop your own web page using HTML, a simple Text program, or a web page editor such as Adobe Dreamweaver®, Amaya, Microsoft Expression Web®, or an online web builder like Google Sites.

Using a Web Editor

➢ You would use a web editor much in the same way you would use a word processor. The single most important capability of a web editor is the ability to create a link.

What is a Link?

➢ A link is a hyper-text or hyper-image that allows the web browser to go to to another part of a web page, or a different web page. You can usually tell where there is a link when your mouse pointer becomes a "hand," or when a line appears below the text.

How do I make a Link?

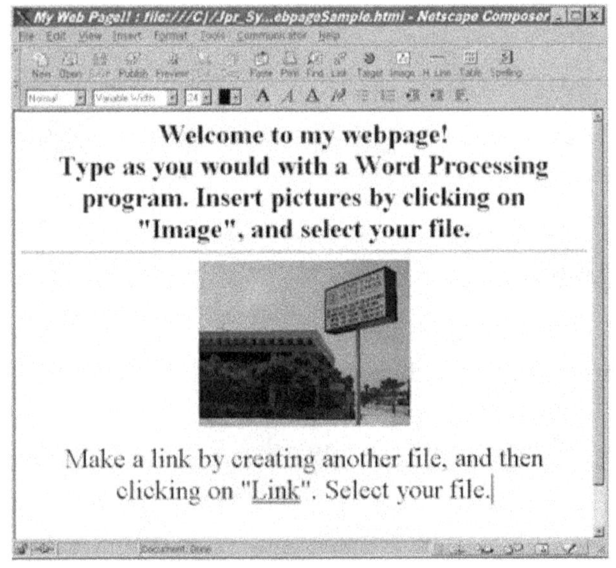

➢ You need to first *select* the text or image you wish make a link, then click on "Link" on the toolbar – you then need to locate the file, or URL (Universal Resource Locator), something like: www.google.com

After you have made your webpage, you need to save it and view it using a web browser: Chrome, Safari®, Firefox®, or Microsoft Internet Explorer®. You can go to *File* and select *Preview in Browser*. If you need to make further changes to your webpage, you need to **go back** to your web page editor..

Class Project # 55
Web Page Design
WWW.PAULRALLION.COM

➢ Write 3 paragraphs about what your webpage is going to be about. Explain the topic you'll cover, why the webpage may be useful, and who your audience is.

Homework # 55
Web Page Design
WWW.PAULRALLION.COM

1.- What is a Webpage Editor used for?
2.- What is the single most important capability of a Webpage Editor?
3.- What is a hyperlink?
4.- Make a LIST of the steps to make a link

Sample Quiz # 55
Web Page Design
WWW.PAULRALLION.COM

1.- What kind of language do web page editors use?
2.- Give the name of one web page editing program:
3.- What allows your browser to go to another part of a web page, or a different web page?
4.- Once you finish your web page, where do you preview it?

Handout # 56

Web Design: Dreamweaver®

WWW.PAULRALLION.COM

Objective: You will learn how to use Dreamweaver® to make your own web page.

What is Macromedia Dreamweaver®?

➢ Dreamwever® is a professional HTML editor used to create webpages. Dreamweaver® allows to either create webpages using a webpage editor: WYSIWYG (what you see is what you get), or using HTML (hyper-text mark-up language) code (programming). When you create a webpage you need to think of a theme for all your pages (files). The file you want people to visit first is called your homepage. You should save that file as: "index.html." All your other files should be linked to and from that index file.

Toolbars

➢ To make your job easier, toolbars are shortcuts from menu commands.

Insert Toolbar:

This toolbar allows you to do common jobs by just clicking on an icon. Click on a different tab to get a different set of tools.

Tip: If the toolbar is not present, go to *Window*, and select: *Insert.*

Properties Toolbar:

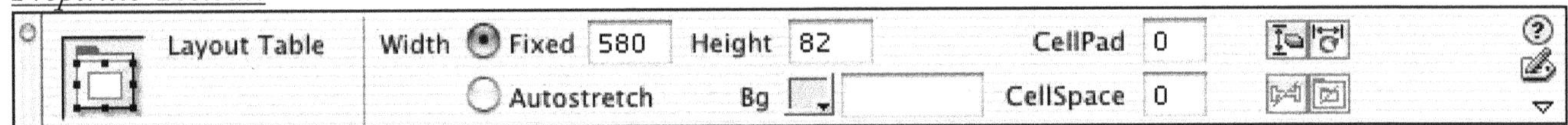

This toolbar allows you to further format your work, according to the insert toolbar. For example, the toolbar above shows "properties" of tables when working on tables. This toolbar will automatically appear when you select the "Tables" tab from the insert toolbar.

Tip: If the toolbar is not present, go to *Window*, and select: *Properties.*

Rollover Images

➢ A rollover image changes when the mouse is placed over it. This adds a nice touch to your webpage. You can find this icon in the "Insert Toolbar" under the "Common" tab. To do Rollover Images you need to have two image files, and a URL you wish people to go to when they click on it. The original image is the image you want to display first, and the rollover image is the image you want people to see when they place the mouse over the picture (without clicking on it).

Class Project # 56

Web Design: Dreamweaver®

WWW.PAULRALLION.COM

➢ Make an index.html page with a title, picture and table of links. For each link, make an .html page about that specific link. You'll end up with five files: index.html, page1.html, page2.html, page3.html, and page4.html. Make sure you link all the pages from and to the index

Homework # 56

Web Design: Dreamweaver®

WWW.PAULRALLION.COM

1.- What is the difference between WYSIWYG and HTML?
2.- If both of your toolbars are NOT present, how do you get them to show?
3.- What are Rollover Images?
4.- How are Rollover Images useful?

Sample Quiz # 56

Web Design: Dreamweaver®

WWW.PAULRALLION.COM

1.- If one of your toolbars doesn't show in Dreamweaver, how do you get it?
2.- What is the command to add a picture to your webpage?
3.- When you pass your mouse over a picture and it changes, it is called:
4.- What should you save your homepage as (include file extension)?

Handout # 57

File Transfer Protocol (FTP)

WWW.PAULRALLION.COM

Objective: You will learn how to upload your files to publish your own web page.

What is ftp?

➤ Students often ask me, "how can I make my html files visible on the Internet?" My answer has to do with this handout's topic. FTP stands for File Transfer Protocol, and it is the standard for a computer to share files with a server online. It is used to upload (and sometimes download) your html, jpg, and other files to your web host servers. Web hosting companies provide storage and access for websites.

Web Hosts:

➤ You pay a monthly or yearly service to your web hosting company. Before hiring a web hosting company, it is a good idea to do some reseach online about their services, offers, and prices. Some examples of Web Host companies are:

iPage eHost.com HostClear ideahost SiteBuilder.com

Uploading files:

➤ After you've secured your web host account you can download a free ftp program and upload your files as show below:

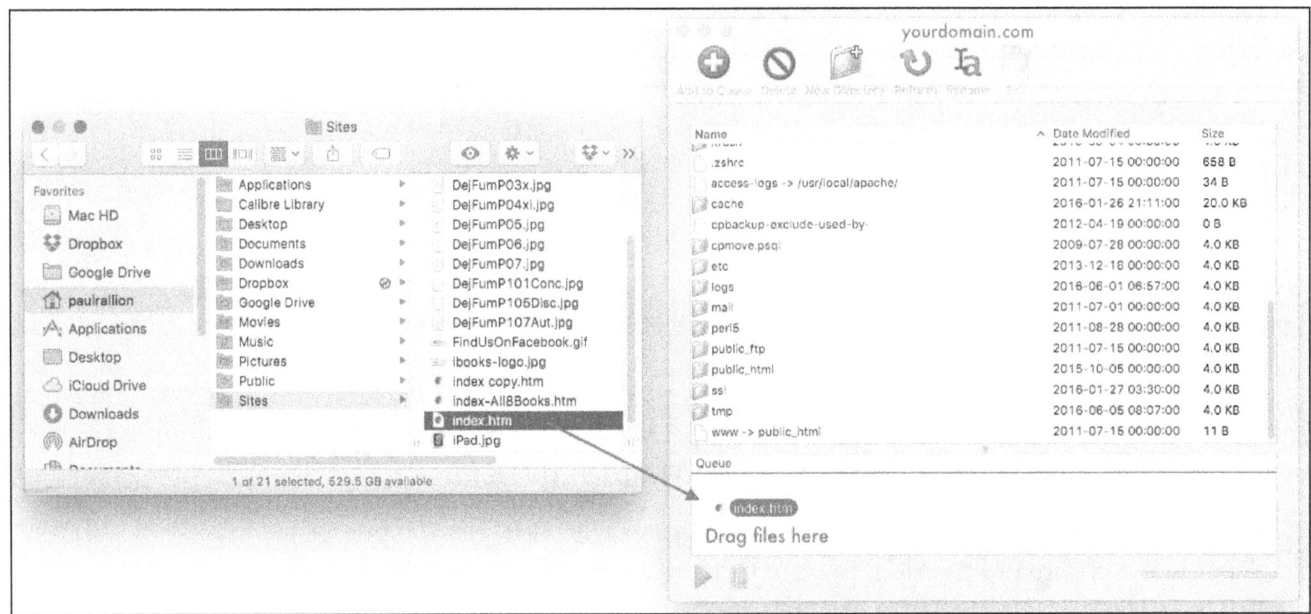

➤ Place your Apple's Finder or Window's Explorer next to your ftp program. Then drag the file(s) from the left and drop them off in the Queue area (following the arrow in the picture above). Done!

Class Project # 57
File Transfer Protocol (FTP)
WWW.PAULRALLION.COM

➢ Make sure that you keep all your web page files in a folder called: Website. When the time comes and you have a web hosting company, get an ftp program and upload your files!

Homework # 57
File Transfer Protocol (FTP)
WWW.PAULRALLION.COM

1.- How can you make your html files visible on the Internet?
2.- What is a web hosting company?
3.- What are some examples of ftp programs?
4.- How do you upload files online?

Sample Quiz # 57
File Transfer Protocol
WWW.PAULRALLION.COM

1.- The protocol for a computer to share files with a server online is:
2.- A company that stores and makes webpages available is called:
3.- What's the easiest way to upload files to a web server?
4.- Which program do you place next to your ftp program to upload files?

Comic Life

WWW.PAULRALLION.COM

Objective: You will learn how to use Comic Life, a program to make your own comic strip.

➢ **Comic Life:** Reading comic strips or comic books is fun, but writing your own comic stories puts you in the driver's seat! Did you just experience a fun event or a great trip? Have you heard a good joke lately? Tell your story with Comic Life! Make an Internet Meme (an image that contains humorous text that is shared online). You can use your scanned pictures or pictures you've taken with your phone or camera and write your own story.

➢ **Templates:**

Just like other programs, you can select from a variety of templates. Select a Page Template based on the story you want to tell, and drag it to the large blank area. You have a drop-down menu from which you can select different themes. Decide how you can divide your story into a sequence of parts. If it helps you, make a quick outline on a piece of paper, or a simple text program, or a word processor. Once you select a page template, add a title. Grab, drag, and drop "Lettering" from the bottom left side of the window and place it on top to type your title.

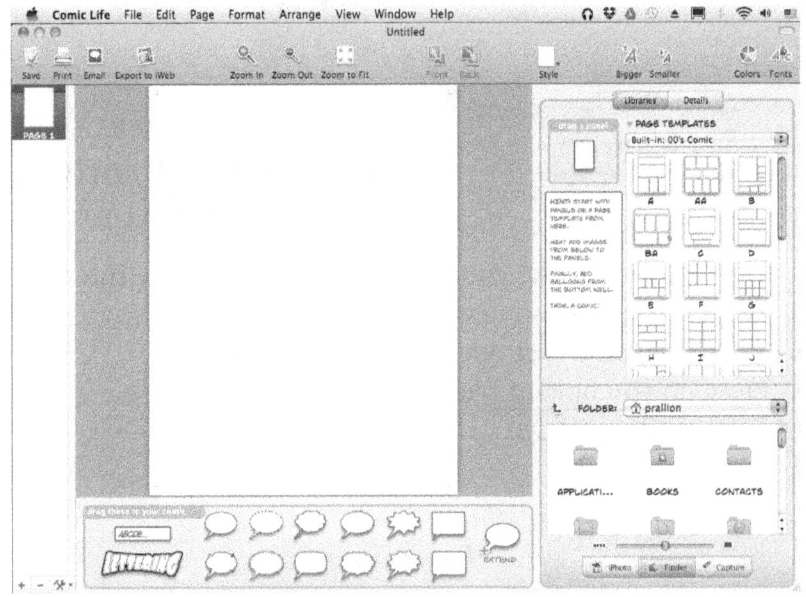

➢ **Adding Stuff:**

For your comic strip you will need pictures, dialogue bubbles and text. Like a regular story, prepare a good "hook," or introduction, keep the story interesting, and prepare a good "punch line," or ending.

* Images:

For images, you have three choices: your iPhoto pictures, your Finder images, or Capture a picture from your computer camera.

* Dialogue Bubbles:

For dialogue bubbles, understand the difference between actual speech bubbles (what your characters say, see 1st image at right) and thoughts, called "thought bubbles" (what your characters think, see 2nd image at right).

* Text:

Click, hold, drag, and drop "Lettering" to your work area, and start typing. You can double-click to change the type of font, size, etc. Enjoy!

Class Project # 58
Comic Life
WWW.PAULRALLION.COM

➢ Using Comic Life, tell a story of your choice: true story, ficticious, funny story, serious, informative, etc. Add pictures, dialogue bubbles, and fancy text.

Homework # 58
Comic Life
WWW.PAULRALLION.COM

1.- What is Comic Life?
2.- How do you add images to your story?
3.- What are dialog bubbles?
4.- How do you add text to your story?

Sample Quiz # 58
Comic Life
WWW.PAULRALLION.COM

1.- In order to get started with Comic Life you need to select a:
2.- To add text to your comic strip, you grab the word:
3.- What kind of dialogue bubbles contain what your characters say?
4.- What kind of dialogue bubbles contain what your characters think?

HANDOUT # 59
Video Editing: iMovie
WWW.PAULRALLION.COM

Objective: You will learn how to edit video and use iMovie to produce your own movies.

What is iMovie®?

➢ iMovie® is a program used to create quick and simple movies, adding titles over video, scene transitions, background music, and voiceovers.

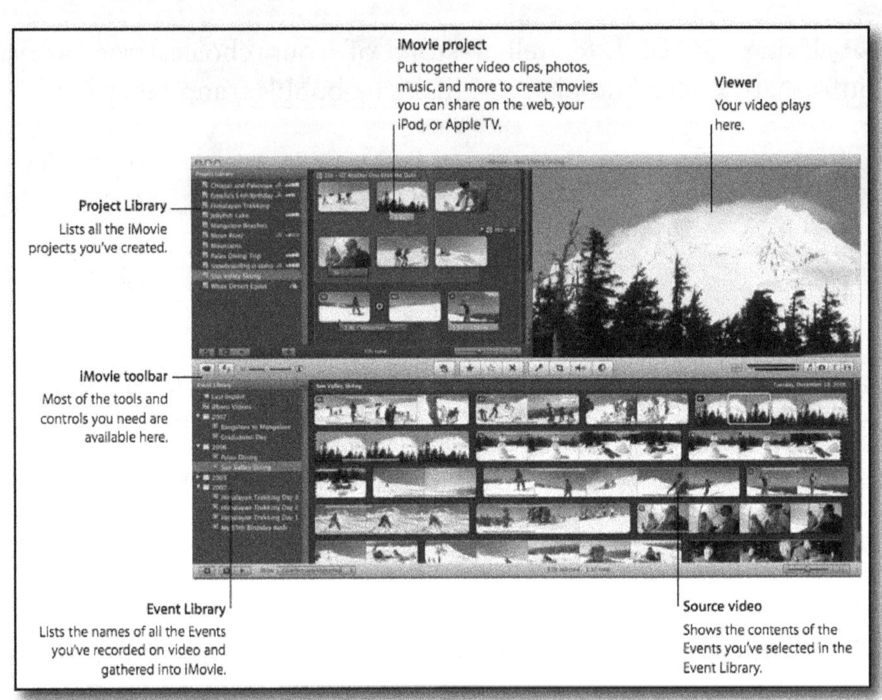

Importing Movies

➢ To import a movie from your digital camera, plug it in to your computer using the USB cable. From the File menu, select Import ⇨ Movies. Move the pointer back and forth across the video to watch it play & get an idea of how the video looks. This is called "Skimming." Click from where you want to begin your new event and drag to the end –you get a yellow selection border, which you can resize. Then drag it to the top left pane to start editing your video.

Adding Music, Photos, Text, Transitions to your Video:

➢ In the Media Browser, you'll find these buttons, in this order:

| *Music* | *Photos* | *Text* | *Transitions* | *Maps/Backgrounds* |
Click *Music* to add a song to your video from your iTunes Library. Click *Photos* to insert a picture. Click *Text* to add a Title. Click *Transitions & Backgrounds* to add a nice touch to your video between video segments.

Video Themes & Effects:

➢ To give your video that professional touch, go to File ⇨ Project Properties. Choose your Theme, and automatically add titles and transitions to your movie! You can edit your titles in the Viewer.

Saving Your Video:

➢ You can save your final work & share it in a few different ways. From the Share menu, select from the following formats to export: iPod, iPhone, iTunes, Apple TV, Computer, even YouTube! To save your movie as an .m4v movie file, click on Share ⇨ Export Movie. Select the video resolution, and the Folder destination to save your file. Enjoy your new movie-making skills!

CLASS PROJECT # 59
Video Editing: iMovie
WWW.PAULRALLION.COM

➢ Use a digital camera to record a short video clip. Import it to iMovie and select a theme: this will add a title and credits to your video.

HOMEWORK # 59
Video Editing: iMovie
WWW.PAULRALLION.COM

1.- How do you import a video clip into iMovie?
2.- What is skimming?
3.- How do you add music, photos, text, and transitions to your video?
4.- How do you save your video?

SAMPLE QUIZ # 59
Video Editing: iMovie
WWW.PAULRALLION.COM

1.- How do you import a video into iMovie?
2.- To get an idea what a video looks like by sliding the pointer back and forth is called:
3.- What is one thing you can add to your movie?
4.- What is the command to save your movie file?

Handout # 60
Flash Animation I
WWW.PAULRALLION.COM

Objective: You will learn how to use Macromedia Flash MX® to make your own animations.

What is Macromedia Flash®?

➤ Macromedia Flash® is a professional program used to create animations. Animations can be frame-by-frame or tweened animations.

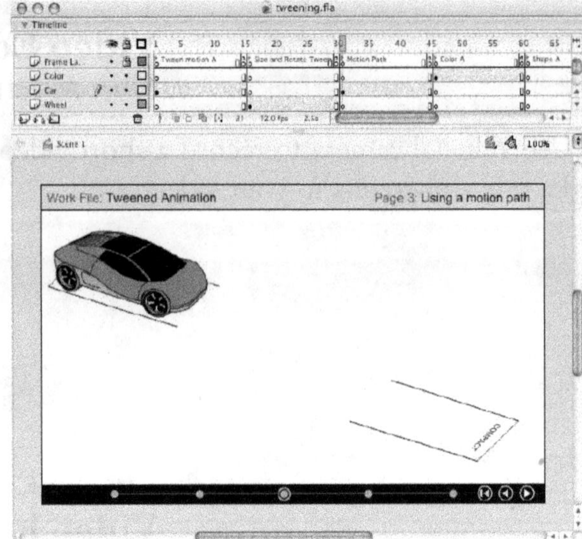

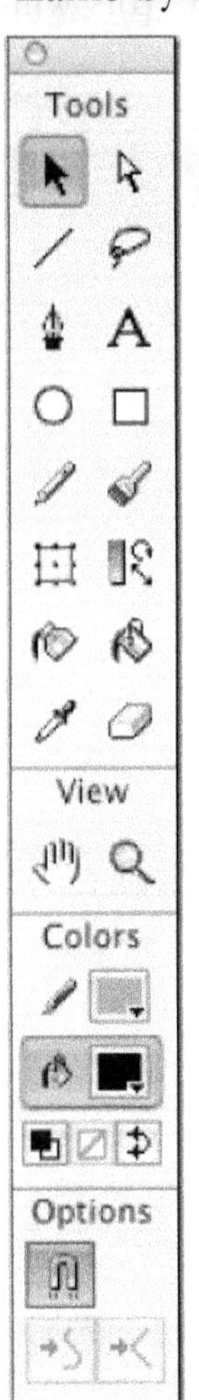

Tweened animations

➤ In tweened animations, you create the starting and ending frames, and you let Flash® create the frames in between. A tween animation will be smaller in file size, therefore it will download faster on your web page.

Steps to make an animation:

➤ These are simple steps you can follow to make your animation with Flash®:

1. Draw any object with the Tools (insert at left) or paste one
2. Highlight Object(s) with arrow tool. If you wish to use text, convert it to symbol.
3. From the *Insert* menu select "*Create Motion Tween.*"
4. Cross-click (or hold down your one-button mouse) anywhere on the timeline (picture below) after frame 1 and click on "Insert Keyframe."
5. Click in last frame number (at the end of arrow) and drag your object to where you want it to move. A keyframe is a frame where you specify changes in an animation.
6. Test your animation (movie) by pressing "Return."

Timeline:

➤ The timeline below shows you all the frames, and where there are changes. Another key element in the timeline is "Layers," which are transparent sheets stacked on top of each other. Layers help organize the contents of your animation. You can draw and make changes to one layer without affecting artwork on another layer. Each layer has its own name, as show below:

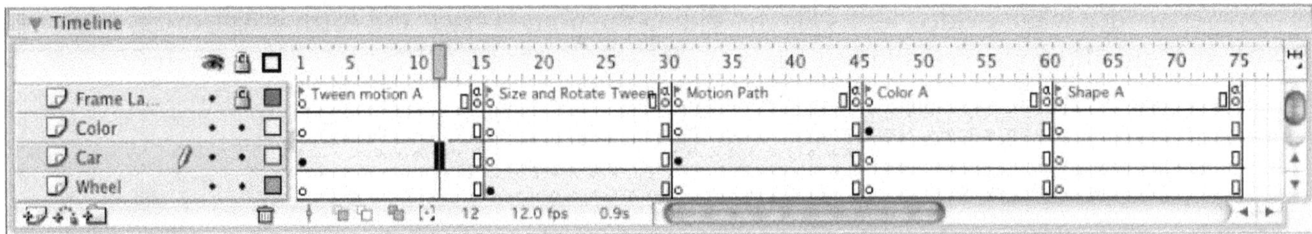

Class Project # 60

Flahs Animation I

WWW.PAULRALLION.COM

➢ Make a simple animation with any object you wish to draw. It can be as basic as stick figures, but you may do fancier drawings.

Homework # 60

Flahs Animation I

WWW.PAULRALLION.COM

1.- What is Macromedia Flash®?
2.- What are tweened animations?
3.- What are the steps to make an animation?
4.- What is the Timeline?

Sample Quiz # 60

Flahs Animation I

WWW.PAULRALLION.COM

1.- What is the name of a professional program used to create animations?
2.- The type of animation where the program creates the frames in between is called:
3.- How do you test your animation once it's finished?
4.- Where can you see all changes and layers?

Handout # 61

Flash Animation II (Frame-by-Frame)

WWW.PAULRALLION.COM

Objective: You will learn how to use Macromedia Flash MX® to make your own animations.

Frame-by-frame animations

➢ In frame-by-frame animations you create the image in every frame. The key factor here is to insert keyframes. Each keyframe is a different transparent "sheet" on which you can draw different images, or a series of images that will give an illusion of motion, i.e.: cartoons. To insert a new keyframe, cross click on the last dot (keyframe), and select "insert keyframe."

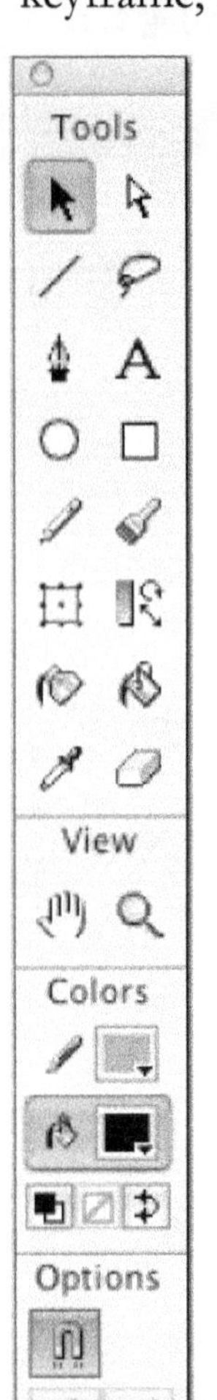

<u>*Layers:*</u>

➢ Sometimes, when you want to change an object, you could alter or change another one by accident. So, it is better to create a new layer so you can lock one layer while you're working on the other. In the figure at right, there are two layers, one "Car" and the other one "Background." If you wish to make a change to one, you can lock the other one; how? click on the lock.

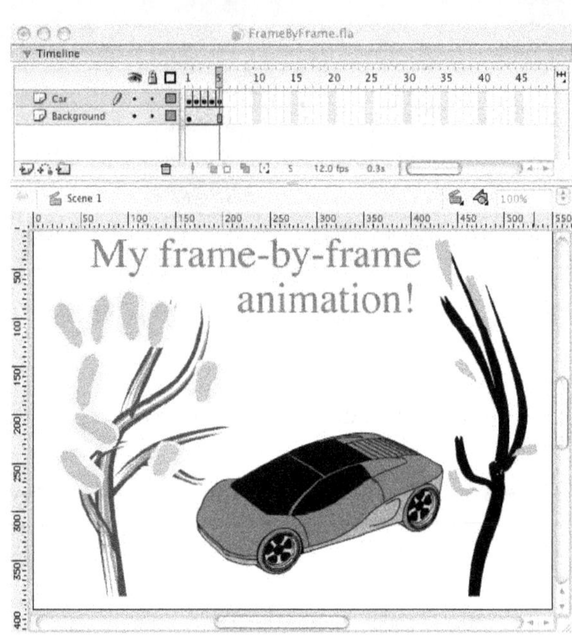

<u>*Animation Timing:*</u>

➢ To control the time of your animation, click in: "fps" frames per second, right under the timeline. You can also change the document's properties, such as document size, and background color.

<u>*Toolbar:*</u>

➢ This toolbar allows you to make any changes to your artwork. Place your mouse over an icon to view its description.

Tip: If the toolbar is not present, go to *Window*, and select: *Tools*.

<u>*Properties Inspector: Text*</u>

➢ This toolbar allows you to format text, just like in any word processing program or drawing program with text capabilities.

Tip: If the toolbar is not present, go to *Window*, and select: *Insert*.

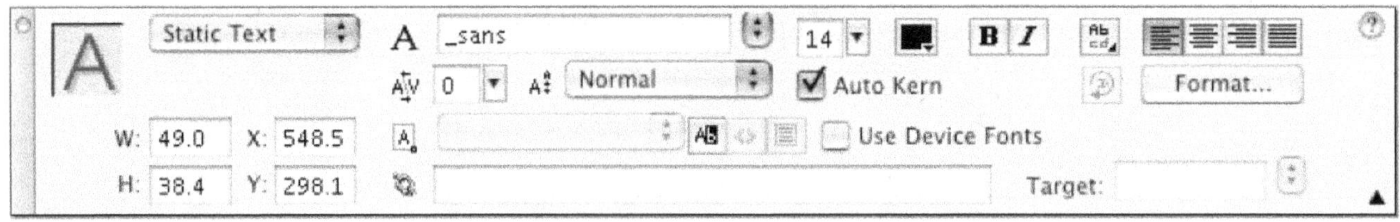

Class Project # 61

Flash Animation II (Frame-by-Frame)

WWW.PAULRALLION.COM

➢ Make a simple animation with any object you wish to draw. It can be as basic as stick figures, but you may do fancier drawings.

Homework # 61

Flash Animation II (Frame-by-Frame)

WWW.PAULRALLION.COM

1.- What are Frame-by-frame animations?
2.- What are Layers?
3.- Explain Animation Timing
4.- How do you get the toolbars to show if they are not present?

Sample Quiz # 61

Flash Animation II (Frame-by-Frame)

WWW.PAULRALLION.COM

1.- What kind of animation do you create the image in every frame?
2.- Transparent sheets are called:
3.- What does "fps" stand for?
4.- What do you do if the toolbars are not present?

Handout # 62
Computer Tips
WWW.PAULRALLION.COM

Objective: You will learn a few tips to make your computing experience more enjoyable.

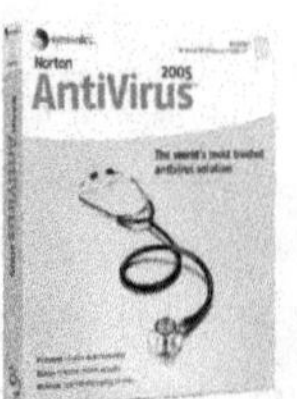

➢ **Antivirus:** A virus is a program that can make your computer run abnormally. You can get a computer virus by opening email attachments, by visiting certain websites, or by sharing storage devices. Many students ask me this: "How can I remove a virus from my computer?" I ask them, "Do you have an antivirus program?" They usually say "no." My advice is to get an antivirus program such as Norton® Antivirus, Microsoft Essentials (for free), etc. and keep it up-to-date by installing its updates! Your internet service provider (ISP) may have a free antivirus program for you.

➢ **Back Up Your Data:** What would you do if you lost all your files today? It is a good idea to double-save your files. You should back them up on a flashdrive or an external hard drive. Macs feature a program called *Time Machine* (picture at right). Go to the Spotlight (top right of your screen) and type Time Machine. Plug in an external hard drive, click Select Disk, and back up!

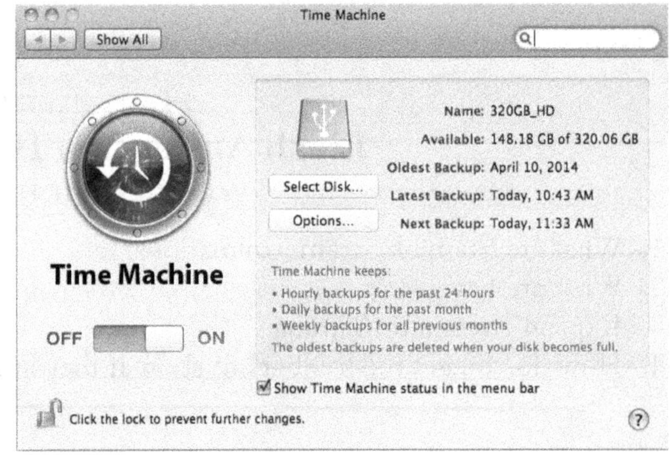

You can also copy files online (on the cloud). You can get a free account at Dropbox.com, a service that syncs your files between your computers, tablets, and smart phones. You no longer need to transfer files between devices with a flash drive or via email. You can also purchase a subscription to an automatic online back-up service such as Carbonite.com.

Other Tips:

➢ Switching Between Open Programs:
A quick way to switch between your open programs is to press and hold "Command" and then press "Tab." This will display the icons of the open programs in the center of the screen (picture at right). Press "Tab" again to select the next icon of your open programs.

➢ Switching Between Open Tabs:
To switch between open tabs within your web browser, press and hold "Control" and then "Tab."

➢ Learning Shortcuts:
To learn shortcuts you can click a menu item on the command bar (at the very top) and it will be displayed on the right hand side of the drop-down menus. They usually start with the "Command" symbol (⌘), followed by a letter. Press and hold the ⌘ key, and then press that letter.

➢ To help your computer run faster: 1) Get as much RAM (Random Access Memory) as possible. *2)* Avoid filling up your hard drive memory capacity. This also applies to your tablet, or smartphone memory capacity. These devices tend to run slower when their memory is full.

Class Project # 62
Computer Tips
WWW.PAULRALLION.COM

➢ Discuss and write about the importance of maintaining an up-to-date anti-virus program and why you should back up your files regularly.

Homework # 62
Computer Tips
WWW.PAULRALLION.COM

1.- Why is an Antivirus program important?
2.- How do you switch between open programs?
3.- What can you do to make your computer run faster?
4.- How can you learn computer shortcuts?

Sample Quiz # 62
Computer Tips
WWW.PAULRALLION.COM

1.- Which program can help you protect your computer?
2.- Which program helps you back up your data on a Mac?
3.- What is your favorite Computer Tip?
4.- What is one thing that can make your computer run faster?

HANDOUT # 63
Computer Maintenance
WWW.PAULRALLION.COM

Objective: You will learn how to keep your computer running in optimal condition.

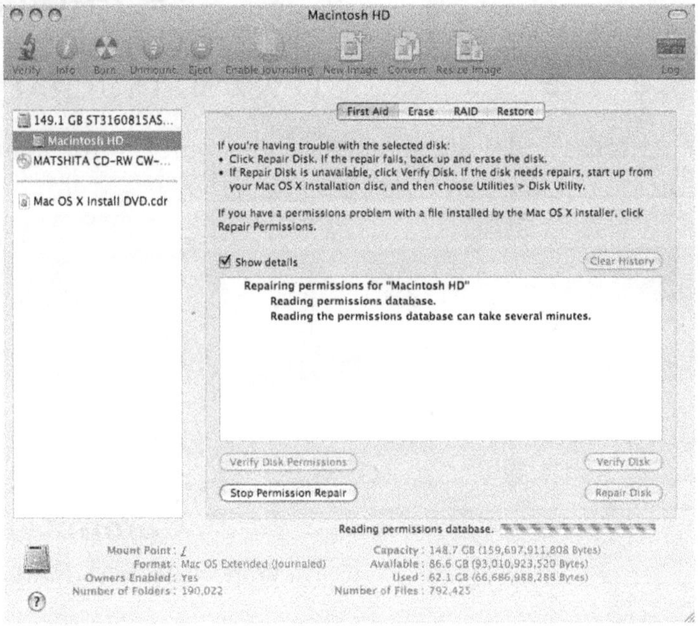

Computer Maintenance (Mac):

➢ According to Apple you don't need to do much to keep your Mac operating smoothly. However, once in a while it's a good idea to "Repair Disk Permissions." Go to the Spotlight (magnifying glass at the very top right corner), and type: "Disk Utility." To start, click your hard drive and click on "Repair Disk Permissions."

Computer Maintenance (Windows):

➢ To keep your Windows computer operating smoothly, you should run two system tools, about once a month. This is how to get to them:

Start ⇨ All Programs ⇨ Accessories ⇨ System Tools ⇨ 1) Disk Cleanup or 2) Disk Defragmenter

1) **Disk Clean Up:** This is a maintenance program that comes with Windows and helps you free up some hard disk space. This utility finds files that are no longer needed, and then gives you the option to remove them.

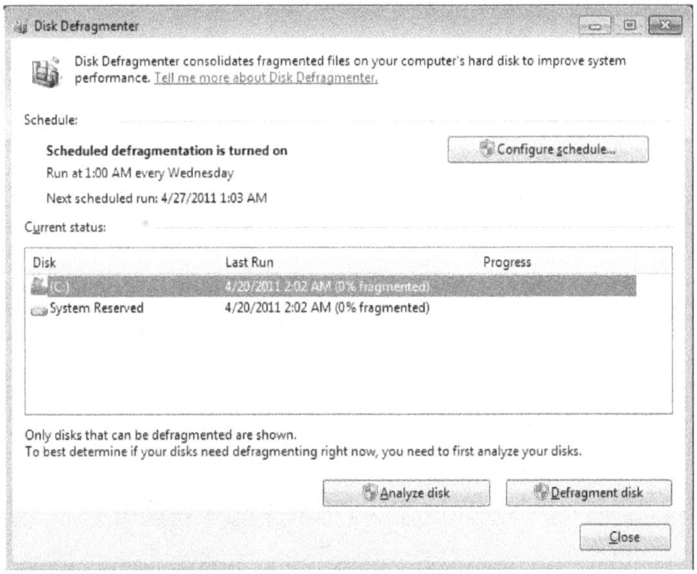

2) **Disk Defragmenter:** This is a maintenance program that comes with Windows and helps your computer rearrange files closer together. This helps the computer find those files faster. Think of how library books are organized. They are organized by genre or by subject area. Imagine if they weren't; a library visitor would have to spend time looking for books all over the place. If files (or books) are well-organized and close together, they're easier to find.

➢ **Run Updates:** No matter which operating system you use, Windows or Apple OS, you should install its updates. They usually contain patches that fix security loopholes, or other important software components.

Class Project # 63
Computer Maintenance
WWW.PAULRALLION.COM

➢ Discuss and write about the importance of performing maintenance on your computer and why you should do it often.

Homework # 63
Computer Maintenance
WWW.PAULRALLION.COM

1.- What is the recommended maintenance for a Mac?
2.- What are the two system tools recommended for Windows?
3.- What is the Disk Defragmenter?
4.- What are Updates?

Sample Quiz # 63
Computer Maintenance
WWW.PAULRALLION.COM

1.- What is one thing you should do occasionally on a Mac?
2.- The system tool that organizes your files on your hard drive for easier access:
3.- The system tool that helps you free up some hard disk space:
4.- Programs that contain patches that fix security loopholes:

HANDOUT # 64
Troubleshooting
WWW.PAULRALLION.COM

Objective: You will learn a few tips to solve some common problems that you may encounter.

Introduction: Computers are great when they work, but they're frustrating when some things don't work. Read these tips and strategies to be better prepared when these things happen.

When Some Things Don't Work:

➢ I Can't Log in? (My Login window shakes)
Sometimes your Log in window might contain 'hidden spaces' entered with the space bar. A quick way to delete those spaces is by pressing the 'Tab' key once, and then the 'Delete' key once.

➢ A Program Doesn't Respond (or Freezes)
When a program freezes on a Mac, there is a quick way to close it: Hold 'Option' and 'Command' keys and then press the 'esc' (escape) key. Select it from the list and click on: "Force Quit." (picture at right)

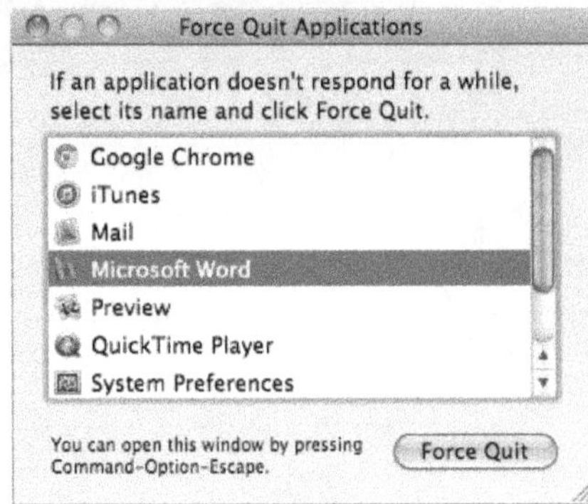

Doing Things Better:

➢ Filling Out Web Forms:
Instead of clicking the next box to continue to fill out information online, press the "Tab" key to move quickly to the next box or rectangle. Hold "Shift" and press "Tab" to navigate backwards.

➢ Active or Inactive Programs:
Even though a computer can have many programs open at the same time, only one program can be active at a time. The screen shot at right shows a word processor open, but it's not active. To make it active, just click anywhere in it. The name of the active program will appear next to the apple menu (top left corner of the screen).

Active Program

➢ File Save vs. File Save As:
File ➪ *Save* allows you to name a file the 1st time you save it, and save it often to keep it updated.
File ➪ *Save As* allows you to create a copy of your saved file with a different name.

➢ Delete vs Backspace:
You can delete text from the beginning or from the end, depending where the cursor is. If the cursor is at the end of a word, press "Backspace." If it is in front of a word, press "Delete."

Class Project # 64
Troubleshooting
WWW.PAULRALLION.COM

➢ Write about and discuss these tips and strategies to be better prepared when these things happen.

Homework # 64
Troubleshooting
WWW.PAULRALLION.COM

1.- How do you know which program is active?
2.- What's an efficient way to fill out web forms?
3.- What do you do when a Mac program doesn't respond?
4.- What's the difference between Delete and Backspace?

Sample Quiz # 64
Troubleshooting
WWW.PAULRALLION.COM

1.- When a program stops working, you can use:
2.- A program whose name appears next to the Apple menu is:
3.- When filling out web forms, how do you move from one box to the next?
4.- To switch programs you press and hold "Command" and then press?

HANDOUT # 65

iTunes & Google Music

WWW.PAULRALLION.COM

Objective: You will learn about iTunes and Google Music to manage your music files.

iTunes:

➤ If you're a music fan, chances are you have an iPod and use iTunes. But how can you create lists of songs defined by certain categories (album, artist, genre, rating, year, etc.) and give them specific titles? These are called *Playlists*, and you'll see how.

Making Playlists:

➤ There are two kinds of Playlists:

Regular: Go to File ➪ New Playlist. Instead of 'untitled playlist,' (in the left pane) give it a name. You need to drag the songs manually from your iTunes Library.

Smart: Go to File ➪ New Smart Playlist. Smart Playlists follow a set of rules that groups your songs together automatically. You can set them up by Album, Artist, etc. For example, if you set up the first drop-down menu as "Rating," the second to "is," and the third to ★★★. Click OK. Instead of 'untitled playlist,' (in the left pane) give it a name, such as "Party." From now on, all songs that you rate with 3 stars should fall into this Smart Playlist, automatically!

➤ Making CD's from iTunes:

Click on the playlist name that you just created and then go to File ➪ Burn Playlist to Disc.

Google Music:

➤ Google Music allows users with a Google account to upload up to 50,000 songs for back up and access online. Go to: music.google.com for more information. You can also create playlists (click the + sign next to "Playlists") and purchase music. Other companies that let you purchase music online may also let you store them on the "Cloud," as a way to back them up for you.

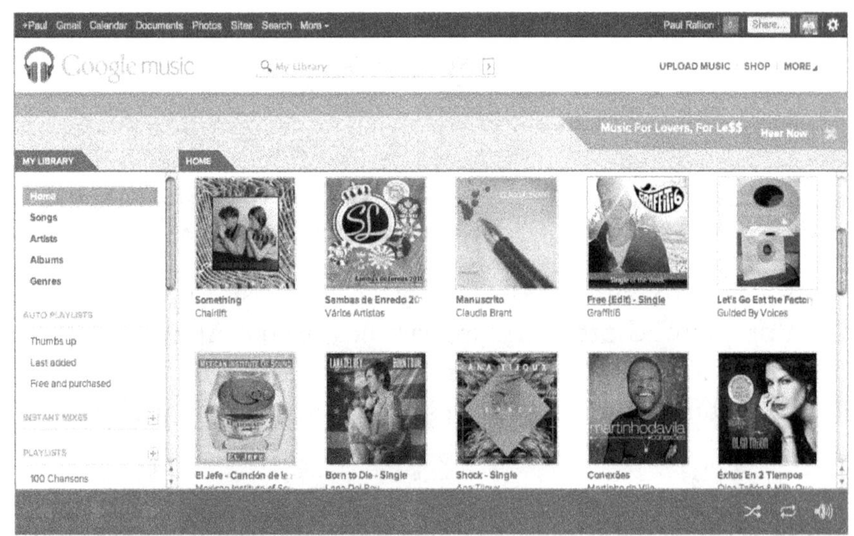

Class Project # 65

iTunes & Google Music

WWW.PAULRALLION.COM

➢ Create a Smart Playlist of songs defined by certain categories: album, artist, genre, rating, year, etc. Try changing the rating on your iPod and watch the Smart Playlist update itself!

Homework # 65

iTunes & Google Music

WWW.PAULRALLION.COM

1.- What are Playlists?
2.- What are the two kinds of Playlists?
3.- How do you burn a CD with iTunes?
4.- What can Google Music do for you?

Sample Quiz # 65

iTunes & Google Music

WWW.PAULRALLION.COM

1.- Lists of songs defined by certain categories are called:
2.- Name one of those categories above:
3.- What kind of playlist arranges your songs automatically given certain conditions?
4.- What service allows you to upload and back up for free up to 20,000 songs?

Handout # 66

How to Take a Screenshot

WWW.PAULRALLION.COM

Objective: You will learn how to take a screenshot of your computer (and smartphone).

Introduction: Taking a screenshot of your computer may have certain advantages. Rather than describing what's on your screen, you can freeze it by way of a picture to show what's on it. Here is how to do it for Mac, Windows, and some smartphones.

➢ ***Macs***: There are three ways you can take a screenshot on your Mac:
1.- The whole screen: Hold the "Command" + "Shift" keys, and then press the number "3."
2.- A part of your screen: Hold the "Command" + "Shift" keys, and then press the number "4." You'll get a crosshair that you can click and drag. Tip: The numbers represent the pixels of your screenshot.
3.- A Window, Desktop, Dock, or the Command menu: Hold the "Command" + "Shift" keys, and then press the number "4," then press the Spacebar. Click when you see the camera.

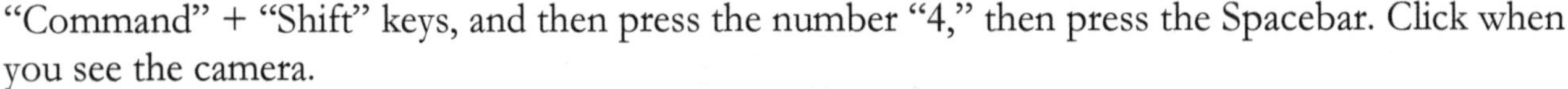

In all cases above, you'll end up with a file on your Desktop named something like: "Screenshot-TodaysDate-CurrentTime." Optional: You can open that file in Preview and crop it by selecting the part of the image you'd like to keep and then go to Tools ⇨ Crop (or "Command" + "K").
Tip: Press the "F11" key to view your Desktop (by hiding all other windows).

➢ ***Windows:*** There are three ways to take a screenshot in Windows:
1.- The whole screen: Press the Print Screen, or "Prt Scn" key.
2.- A part of your screen: Use the Snipping Tool.
3.- The Active Window: Press the "Alt" + "Prt Scn" key.
For cases 1 and 3 above, open the "Paint" program and paste your picture there by going to Edit ⇨ Paste, or by pressing the "Ctrl" + "V" keys. You can also open other programs where "Paste" is allowed and place the screenshot there, since PrtScrn places the image on the clipboard.

➢ ***Bonus*** – You can take a screenshot of your smartphone's and tablet's screen*.

Apple's iOS:

Press both the "Home" and "Sleep" buttons at the same time. The screen will flash for a second. The same procedure works for iPads.

Android:

Go to Settings and find "Palm Swipe to Capture." Move your hand across the screen and wait for the shutter sound. The same procedure works for Android tablets.

* Note: In both cases above, your picture is saved in the "Camera Roll."
Unfortunately, this may or may not work with certain phones or tablets.

Class Project # 66
How to Take a Screenshot
WWW.PAULRALLION.COM

➢ Take various screenshots using the different methods. Save it to your flashdrive. Name them accordingly. Use them as needed: email, add to a report, etc.

Homework # 66
How to Take a Screenshot
WWW.PAULRALLION.COM

1.- Why would you need to take a screenshot?
2.- How do you take a screenshot in Windows?
3.- How do you take a screenshot in Mac?
4.- How do you take a screenshot with the cell phone of your choice?

Sample Quiz # 66
How to Take a Screenshot
WWW.PAULRALLION.COM

1.- What is one advantage of taking a screenshot?
2.- What is ONE way to take a screenshot in Mac?
3.- What is ONE way to take a screenshot in Windows?
4.- Taking a screenshot of a tablet is the same as its cell phone relative. True or False?

Handout # 67
How to Buy a Computer
WWW.PAULRALLION.COM

Objective: You will learn a few tips about purchasing a computer.

Computer Specifications: ➢ There are many computers out there, so which one do I buy? The answer has to do with budget and preference. Don't buy the most expensive computer as it may soon become obsolete. Instead, plan on getting a new computer every three years. Three things to focus on: microprocessor, RAM memory, and hard disk capacity.

⇨ **Microprocessor:** This is the chip that controls most of the PC, so it is important. Get an Intel Pentium. Stay away from other, less powerful processors, such as Intel Celeron. If it is MMX it will help speed up a few of the things you may be doing, such as playing games and video clips. MMX is designed to accelerate multimedia and communications applications.

⇨ **Memory:** Be generous when buying memory, also known as RAM (random-access memory). It determines the capacity for manipulating data – like Web pages– at any given moment. Get at least 4 gigabytes (GB)!

⇨ **Hard Disk:** This is the computer's long-term memory for programs and documents, so it should be as roomy as possible, especially to accomodate your music collection, photos, and videos on your computer. Get at least 320 GB!

➢ ***Laptops:*** As of this writing, more laptops are sold than desktop computers. Initially, the biggest limitation of laptops was their capacity. Now with RAM and hard drives of large capacity PLUS portability and remote access, you really don't need a desktop computer. Who needs to be stationary, when you can bring your laptop to your backyard, to a café with Wi-Fi, or even on an airplane?

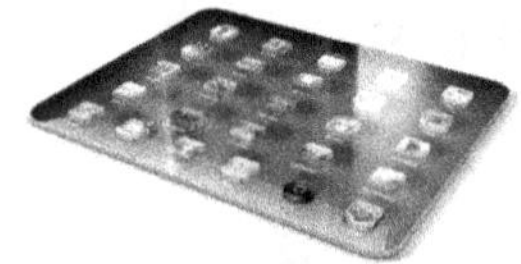

➢ ***Tablets:*** This wave of electronic devices could be placed somewhere between smart-phones and laptops. Yet, they are neither –too big to talk on and too small to be a full-fledged computer. Portability is one of the top advantages, and the list of things they let you do is amazing: read/write email, surf the web, read books, text, video chat, take pictures, sync calendar, contacts, etc. The limit is in the amount of "apps" or programs you can install and run on these amazing machines.

➢ ***Mac or Windows?*** Macs use higher-end processors and materials. They usually have less trouble in the long run and their battery lasts longer. Windows PC's are less expensive, which means you could buy a new laptop more often. In general, your choice between Mac or Windows comes down to budget and preference.

Class Project # 67
How to Buy a Computer
WWW.PAULRALLION.COM

➢ Work in pairs. One student will pretend to be a computer salesperson while the other, the buyer. Act out a computer purchasing scenario. What questions would you ask?

Homework # 67
How to Buy a Computer
WWW.PAULRALLION.COM

1.- What are three things to focus on when buying a computer?
2.- What is RAM?
3.- What is the difference between laptops and tablets?
4.- What do you prefer, Mac or PC? Why?

Sample Quiz # 67
How to Buy a Computer
WWW.PAULRALLION.COM

1.- What is the chip that controls most of the PC?
2.- What determines the capacity for manipulating data at any given moment?
3.- What's the name of the device between a smartphone and a laptop?
4.- It is impossible to generate a PDF file from a Windows machine. True or False?

Discussion Notes

I hope you enjoyed reading about and using some of the programs and techniques presented in this collection of handouts. Maybe you discovered new ways of doing things or received validation for things you already do with your computer.

• **If you're a teacher:** I hope you can use in your classroom some of the information presented in this book. Maybe you discovered new applications for some of the programs you already use.

• **If you're a parent:** I hope these handouts helped you explore and enjoy your computer more. With this information, you can help your child(ren) learn more about computer applications.

• **If you're a student:** I hope you found these handouts interesting and that you found different ways of doing things with your computer. One of the most innovative concepts is the application of Google Docs which will help you collaborate with other students without having to meet in person.

• **If you're a professional in another field:** I hope you liked the computer concepts and applications that are taught in school. I also hope you have found this book educational as well as entertaining.

Please do not hesitate to contact me with your feedback at paulrallion@gmail.com
For more information, please visit my web page at: www.paulrallion.com

Conclusion

I have shared with the reader a wide range of computer applications which I teach at the middle school level and some of it I taught at the adult education level. I started with computer basics, to drawing and painting with a computer, digital imaging, productivity software (including Google Docs), the Internet (web design, email), computer tips, video and music software, etc.

As in real life, the best way to learn something is to practice. Read this book all the way through, and then do the projects and homework after each handout and refer back to the handouts if necessary. Afterwards, try to answer the quizzes without looking at the handouts.

Although some programs are unique in what they can do, there is more than one way of doing things. The handouts presented here are limited to one sheet each. Therefore, they cannot possibly contain everything there is to know about a given program. Go online and do some research. Explore, learn shortcuts, get used to the programs that you need or like.

A few years ago it was more complicated to purchase a new computer. With the gap between Mac and Windows becoming smaller, it has pretty much come down to how much money you want to spend. But no matter what kind of computer you buy, make sure you get an anti-virus program, run updates, and do the recommended maintenance to keep it in good shape.

Acknowledgements

I wish to extend my appreciation to three school administrators who trusted me and gave me the opportunity to teach Computer Technology at the three different levels: Ms. Rita Caldera at the elementary level, Ms. Veronica Aragon at the middle school level, and Ms. Claudine Ajeti at the adult education level.

Authors' Note

Writing this book has been a reflective journey that took me back to when I started typing my first handout. It has given me the chance to relive some of my interesting experiences in the computer lab. I have enjoyed putting these handouts together to share with my students, and other teachers who have inquired about computer concepts or applications. With this book, I am making my handouts available to you. As the subtitle of the book suggests, *The Computer Book for Everyone*, I am sharing these computer concepts with the general public.

By no means do I consider myself the absolute expert computer user. In fact, I pride myself on my willingness to learn and grow as a human being and teacher. As computer technology continues to advance, I hope to continue to improve my own repertoire. It is my duty to stay current with emerging technologies as I cannot stop learning. My students, in turn, enjoy my class, and it is highly rewarding seeing students learn about technology and use it wisely.

Finally, I would like to thank you, the reader. I hope that you have enjoyed these handouts as well as the projects, homework, and quizzes. I hope this book can earn a place in the reference section of your personal library.

If any of these handouts have been of special interest or help to you, please do not hesitate to contact me with your feedback. My e-mail address is paulrallion@gmail.com.

About the Author

Paul Rallion

I was born and grew up in El Salvador. My dad was a French engineer and my mom was a housewife. I worked as an applications engineer in the mid 1990's. I obtained my teaching credential and my master's degree in education in 2003, and achieved National Board Certification in 2006. I became a Google Educator in 2014.

I have worked in the field of education, first as a teacher's assistant, then as a computer lab and science lab instructor. I have taught science, math, and now computer technology. I also taught English as a Second Language (ESL) and then Computer Literacy to adults at night school.

In 2009 I co-authored the book, Middle Schoolin', 50 Stories about the Challenges, Humor, and Rewards of Teaching.
In 2011 I wrote the book, Kick Smokin' One Butt at a Time. The book is available in:
Spanish: Deja de fumar, Un cigarrillo a la vez,
French: Arrête de fumer, Une cigarette à la fois,
Portuguese: Deixe de fumar, Um cigarro de cada ves.
In 2012, I co-authored the book, Turning Point, Free Education for the Willing.
In 2014 I wrote Middle School 101, 101 Tips for Teachers.

For more information, please visit my web site: www.paulrallion.com

---

Glossary

➤ Here are a few abbreviations that appear frequently:

CPU: Central Processing Unit

ISP: Internet Service Provider

PDF: Portable Document Format

RAM: Random Access Memory

ROM: Read-Only Memory

USB: Universal Serial Bus

URL: Universal Resource Locator

WWW: World Wide Web

Units of Data:

Byte: Storage unit of data

1 Kilobyte (KB): 1,000 Bytes

1 Megabyte (MB): 1,000 KB

1 Gigabyte (GB): 1,000 MB

1 Terabyte (TB): 1,000 GB

1 Petabyte (PB): 1,000 TB

Web Resources

Here are a few useful web sites:

www.apple.com Apple Computer Official Site.

www.google.com Google Corporation Official Site.

www.microsoft.com Microsoft Official Site.

www.goodtyping.com Online Typing Course.

www.paulrallion.com My personal Site.

Note: Screenshots have been taken from the programs featured in this book.

Keyboard Shortcuts

➢ Here are 10 Computer Shortcuts popular in both Mac and Windows:

Mac:	Windows:
1. Command ⌘ + N = New Document	1. Alt + F, then N = New Document
2. Command ⌘ + W = Close Window	2. Alt + F, then W = Close Window
3. Command ⌘ + S = Save	3. Ctrl + S = Save
4. Command ⌘ + P = Print	4. Ctrl + P = Print
5. Command ⌘ + Z = Undo last step(s)	5. Ctrl + Z = Undo last step(s)
6. Command ⌘ + Y = Redo last step(s)	6. Ctrl + Y = Redo last step(s)
7. Command ⌘ + C = Copy	7. Ctrl + C = Copy
8. Command ⌘ + V = Paste	8. Ctrl + V = Paste
9. Command ⌘ + A = Select All	9. Ctrl + A = Select All
10. Command ⌘ + F = Find	10. Ctrl + F = Find

➢ Delete full words instead of one letter at a time (both Mac and Windows):
For Mac: place the cursor after the word you would like to delete, press and hold "Option," and press Delete. It also works with forward delete: fn + Option + Delete. For Windows, use "Ctrl."

➢ To type accents and ñ's:
- For Windows: First, you need to set up a US-International keyboard. Follow these steps: Control Panel ⇨ Clock, Language, Region ⇨ Regional & Language Options ⇨ Change Keyboards or other input methods ⇨ Change Keyboards ⇨ General tab: Select English (United States) - United States - International. Click OK. *You only need to do this once.*
To type an accent: type the ' key and then the letter. To type the ñ, type the ~ key and then the n.

- For Mac: Press and hold "Option," and the letter "e" key, then type the letter you wish accented. For ñ, press and hold "Option," and the letter "n" key, then type the letter "n" again.

References:

1. Patti Winters; Patrick Winters; Richard Moore; Cambridge Educational (Firm). The history of computers (DVD video, 2008). Lawrenceville, NJ : Cambridge Educational, 2008.

2. Google for Education: www.google.com/edu/

3. Free typing course online: www.goodtyping.com

www.ingramcontent.com/pod-product-compliance
Lightning Source LLC
Chambersburg PA
CBHW080421060326
40689CB00019B/4326
* 9 7 8 1 1 0 5 5 6 0 2 9 3 *